THE
QUAKER
BIBLE
READER

EDITED BY

PAUL BUCKLEY &

STEPHEN W. ANGELL

The Quaker Bible Reader

Copyright © 2006 by Earlham School of Religion Publications, a division of Earlham Press, 228 College Avenue, Richmond, IN 47374.

Library of Congress Cataloguing-In-Publication Data

Buckley, Paul, 1949-

Angell, Stephen W. 1952-

The Quaker Bible Reader / Paul Buckley and Stephen W. Angell

ISBN 978-1-879117-16-7

Library of Congress Control Number: 2005939133

1. Bible—Criticism, Interpretation, etc. 2. Quakerism

DEDICATED WITH GREAT FONDNESS TO
T. CANBY JONES

CONTENTS

ACKNOWLEDGEMENTS

A project such as this always requires the support of many, many people. In addition to the chapter authors, we wish to acknowledge the contributions of (in alphabetical order) Paul Anderson, Michael Birkel, Nancy Bowen, Ernie Buscemi, Adriana Cabrera-Velasquez, Marty Grundy, Doug Gwyn, T. Canby Jones, Anthony Manousos, Jay Marshall, Barbara Mays, Trayce Peterson, Tim Seid, Krystin Schmidt, Daniel Smith-Christopher, Peggy Spohr, and Sandra Ward-Angell.

You may not know what you did for us, but we thank you.

Special thanks are due to Dr. Pierre Jolicoeur for allowing us to use "The Reader" on the cover.

Paul Buckley is known among Friends for his work with various Quaker organizations and for his articles and workshops on the history, faith, and practice of the Religious Society of Friends. In 1998, he undertook a mid-life career change and earned a MA in Quaker Studies at the Earlham School of Religion. His books include *Twenty-First Century Penn*, a translation of five of William Penn's theological works into modern English, and *Owning the Lord's Prayer*, a meditation on that prayer. Paul lives in Indianapolis with his beautiful wife, Peggy. He has three amazing adult children and one astounding granddaughter.

INTRODUCTION

Paul Buckley

In May 2004, I had a fateful conversation with Steve Angell. Among other things, we talked about our current projects. I told Steve that I had been struggling for several years with the idea that Friends—especially those in the more liberal meetings—needed a book on how to read the Bible and that I was supposed to do it. Although I was convinced that God was calling me to the project, it was stalled and I saw no prospect of getting it moving any time soon. Steve's comment was, "Maybe you're not supposed to do it alone." In a flash, I knew he was right. There isn't just one way for a Quaker to read scripture. While other religious bodies might have a single, approved set of rules for interpretation, the theological, spiritual, and ethnic diversity within the Religious Society of Friends has spawned an equally wide variety of approaches to scripture—approaches that are outwardly different, but each firmly rooted in Quaker faith and practice.

No one Quaker could write such a book—even two or three are inadequate. Only a broad collection of writers could represent the many, diverse techniques that Friends have developed for reading scripture. In the next few minutes, we had sketched a plan for this book and drawn up a list of more than twenty potential authors from all branches of Friends we would have liked to participate. What you are now holding is the result.

The Bible Among Friends

For many Friends, the Bible is a lost resource. They don't read it, and they don't miss it. This is not a new situation—complaints that too few Friends read or know scripture have been heard consistently for at least the last two-hundred years. For example, more than fifty years ago, Henry Cadbury, a Quaker and one of the twentieth century's great biblical scholars, decried this condition in an address at Guilford College.[1]

In some ways, this is a surprising situation. Friends in the seventeenth century were devoted to their Bibles. Early Quaker writings seem at times to consist of little more than stringing together selected bits from scripture. George Fox, founder of the Religious Society of Friends, knew scripture so well that Gerard Croese, in his 1696 book, *The General History of the Quakers*, makes the claim that "though the Bible were lost, it might be found in the *Mouth* of *George Fox.*" Early Friends, of course, were not unique in their love of the scriptures. Three hundred and fifty years ago, the Bible was the pre-eminent book in the English-speaking world. For many people, it was the only readily accessible book and it profoundly influenced views of life, society, history, politics, and the world. George Fox was far from unique in committing it to memory.

Despite this intimate familiarity with the Bible, the tension between the roles of immediate revelation and of

---

[1] Cadbury, Henry J. *A Quaker Approach to the Bible.* The Ward Lecture, Guilford College, Guilford, NC, on November 9, 1953.

scripture has been present from the very earliest beginnings of the Quaker movement. In the section of his *Journal* devoted to 1648, George Fox wrote:

> I was to direct people to the Spirit that gave forth the Scriptures, by which they might be led into all Truth, and so up to Christ and God, as they had been who gave them forth. ... I saw that the grace of God, which brings salvation, had appeared to all men, and that the manifestation of the Spirit of God was given to every man to profit withal. These things I did not see by the help of man, nor by the letter, though they are written in the letter, but I saw them in the light of the Lord Jesus Christ, and by his immediate Spirit and power... for I was in that Spirit by which they [the scriptures] were given forth, and what the Lord opened to me I afterwards found was agreeable to them. I could speak much of these things and many volumes might be written but all would prove too short... (p. 34)

Fox is claiming immediate revelation for himself and declaring his mission to be directing all people to know it in themselves. The final sentence makes it clear that these revelations are more than a mere reiteration of the recorded scriptures. At the same time, he acknowledges that *afterward* he found that what had been revealed to him was "agreeable" with scripture. This formulation— continuing revelation that does not contradict (but may go beyond) the Bible became the Quaker norm and appears in the writings of many other early Friends. The evolving structures of gospel order did little to provide precise definitions of what was agreeable and what contradicted scripture. In general, it was left to subgroups within the Society—monthly, quarterly, and yearly meetings—to deal with individual cases. This process led to a degree of local conformity, but no Society-wide standard.

This tension remained unresolved at the beginning of the nineteenth century. If anything, the cracks were widening as ideas were absorbed both from the Enlightenment and from other Protestant sects. The events leading up to painful separations in the Society in 1827-28 prominently featured charges and countercharges over how the Bible was read, how it should be read, and how it was properly interpreted—although not over its ultimate status among Friends. Of course, each side claimed proper use for themselves and charged serious error on the part of their opponents.

Nor are the 1820s unique in this respect. Today's structures, organizations, and practices within the Religious Society of Friends are the product of our history. It is only a slight exaggeration to say that it is impossible to understand Quaker history without having some understanding of Quaker theology and impossible to understand Quaker theology without knowing something of the Bible. The peace testimony, the practice of simplicity, both silent worship and the elements of programmed worship, and the other hallmarks of twenty-first century Quaker faith and practice were firmly established on biblical foundations.

Even understanding the ways we speak of ourselves depends on scripture. Many contemporary Friends take pleasure in referring to themselves as belonging to a "peculiar people." But to say we are "peculiar" is not to claim that we are odd. The phrase is found in both the Hebrew (Old Testament) and Greek (New Testament) scriptures. As a Quaker, my favorite example is from the first epistle of Peter, "But ye are a chosen generation, a royal priesthood, an holy nation, a peculiar people; that ye should shew forth the praises of him who hath called you out of darkness into his marvellous light" (1 Peter 2:9). We Quakers are well acquainted with that "marvellous light." This is, of course, the translation in the King James Version of the Bible. In modern English versions, "peculiar people" is rendered as "a people belonging to God" or "God's own people." To say we are a peculiar people is to claim that the Religious Society of Friends is the chosen people.

Early Friends indeed made this claim, but we shouldn't think it was a point of pride. They knew the implications of being God's people—it may be an honor, but it is much more a responsibility. To know the elements of that responsibility, you need look no further than the historic Quaker testimonies. Early Friends described the testimonies as "peculiarities," but not to suggest these were mere idiosyncrasies. These are the obligations that God's people carry. A person adopted Quaker dress, speech, and practices as an outward sign of submission to God in all things.

Reasons Quakers Don't Read the Bible

Modern Quakers do not neglect books in general. Professionally, Friends are found in academic and other intellectual professions well out of proportion to their numbers in the population. In any moderately sized collection of Quakers, there is likely to be at least one librarian. Nor are Friends uninterested in spiritual matters. A quick review of the materials offered in the various Quaker bookstores reveals long lists of books on spirituality, Quaker biography, other religious biographies, devotionals, guides to spiritually-based social action, and a variety of religious study materials for all ages. But listening to conversations, especially among more liberal Friends, might give the impression that more copies are sold of Gnostic gospels than those of Matthew, Mark, Luke, and John.

While the Bible used to enjoy a privileged position in the English-speaking world, today's world is vastly different. Even beyond the constant and unavoidable impingements of non-print media in our lives, the competition for a reader's attention is enormous. Our lives are flooded with books, newspapers, magazines, catalogs, mail, email, text-messages, and more. In modern America, discarded printed material is the single largest source of consumer garbage. As a spiritual resource, the Bible competes with abundant other sources, from traditional writings to the products of self-help gurus. Within the category of sacred works, the Bible now shares shelf space with the scriptures of other religions. This diminished role makes itself apparent in everyday life. While in the seventeenth century, scriptural quotes and allusions were the commonplace of daily conversation and literary works, today's popular culture recycles lines from songs, jingles, slogans, and advertising.

Competition with other resources aside, however, I believe one of the principal reasons many Friends do not read the Bible is they do not have any idea how to approach the Bible *as Quakers*. Some have never been introduced to it. Others may have learned at an earlier time in their lives to read the Bible in a particular way. For various reasons, they have come to reject that way of reading and, in rejecting the interpretation, they have thrown the text out with it.

Many people had their first encounter with the Bible in a Sunday School (or, as Quakers call it, a First Day School) class. In this setting, the stories are reformulated to present a simple lesson for a young mind. Complexity is rooted out, and a single, simple message—appropriate to a child's understanding—is emphasized. Only a small sampling of the whole is presented: Adam and Eve, the flood, Moses parting the sea, and Jesus feeding thousands with a few loaves and fishes are popular; Joshua conquering the Canaanites and the vivid images in the Apocalypse are not. There are implicit or explicit theological assumptions underlying the selection and rewording of Bible stories, but these are invisible to a child. In fact, a young child hearing a Bible story is not likely to be taught that there is any interpretation involved. Children do not interpret stories, they just listen to them. It would never occur to them to deconstruct Dr. Seuss, so why should they treat Bible stories any differently? As he or she grows, such hidden assumptions may or may not become more apparent. In any case, they are often very different from the theological assumptions and beliefs that an older child or adult holds. For some, it is easy to believe that, just as they no longer read picture books, they have likewise outgrown the Bible.

Other Friends learned to read scripture within another faith community before coming into our Society. This may mean reading the Bible as literally and infallibly true or as a book to be understood only in light of church traditions and teachings. (Being brought up Catholic, I fall into the latter category.) The distinction between the words of scripture and the meanings ascribed to those words is often lost. Leaving one spiritual community for another entails giving up certain beliefs, perhaps including those about how to read scripture. Where text and interpretation have been thoroughly entwined, it may seem to a newly-convinced Quaker that the Bible can no longer speak to his or her spiritual condition. The God who directed the flood (at least as they were previously taught) cannot be the God who leads them to embrace the peace testimony.

Special attention is due to those who tell you that they have been "wounded by scripture." I have frequently heard women, people of color, poor people, gay men, and lesbians refer to instances when various passages have been used to attack, demean, and belittle them. Over the years, the Bible's words have been used to justify verbal, spiritual, emotional, and physical violence. These attacks do not always issue from the mouths of bigots or intransigent reactionaries, but may come from loving, kind people who were taught "the right way to read the Bible." In response, many of those who have felt so assaulted have denied the validity of the claims made in the name of the Bible. Others, however, accept their attackers' interpretation as a true reflection of the scriptures themselves. They then see themselves as faced with a stark choice: to deny themselves or to deny the validity of the book. It is no surprise that many of these people have chosen to turn away from the scripture.

Others see the Bible as no more than a set of legends and fables, offering insight into the minds of an ancient people and a foreign culture—much like *Beowulf* or *Aesop's Fables*. The Bible presents western civilization's myths, but for truth about the world we live in, they turn to science. Or they may look at the rich variety of other spiritual books and question the special status accorded to the Bible. Why, they ask, grant it pride of place instead of reading the Koran or the Upanishads or the sacred works of the Druids?

The Goal of this Book

It may be useful at this point to introduce one technical term: hermeneutics. Every time someone tells a Bible story, they are engaged—consciously or not—in interpretation. There is a set of rules that they use to ferret out the meaning of a text. For example, while "serpent" may just be a fancy name for a snake, to many people the serpent that tempted Eve into eating forbidden fruit is more than a common snake—but what? Some will tell you the serpent is a devil in disguise. This interpretation contributes to and supports a particular meaning for the story. Others consider the role of the serpent as minor and come to very different conclusions. Each set of rules—implicit or explicit, known or subconscious—constitutes what Bible scholars call hermeneutics.

There is no one set of Quaker hermeneutics. As will be seen in the chapters that follow, there are a number of techniques and approaches to understanding scripture that are consistent with Quaker beliefs and practices. I hope that this book will provide readers with a sense of the varieties of Quaker hermeneutics—assorted, Friendly ways to read and understand scripture. But this isn't the goal of the book. As Manuel Guzman-Martínez says, "Unfortunately, no one learns in someone else's shoes." Our goal is to help you find your own shoes and put them on.

Finding the "Quaker hermeneutics" that speak to your spiritual condition may allow you to engage the Bible in an honest conversation. Then you, too, can do "Quaker exegesis"—not passively accepting someone else's interpretation; not looking for "the good parts" and skipping the rest; not contorting scripture to support predetermined ideas—but entering into a dialogue with this ancient book, exploring your own assumptions about God, and deepening your relationship with the divine. In the process, I believe you will also come to have a more grounded understanding of who Quakers are and why we believe what we believe.

THE
QUAKER
BIBLE
READER

Don Smith was born in Ann Arbor, Michigan, in 1970. Introduced to Quakerism at fourteen, he quickly came to see it as the spiritual home he had been missing. For the last 10 years, he has been active in Religious Education of Young Friends in New England and Lake Erie Yearly Meetings. He twice served as a counselor for YouthQuake, and was the co-coordinator of the FGC High School Program in 2003 and 2004. Don received a doctorate in Astrophysics from the Massachusetts Insititute of Technology in 1999 and in 2005 became a Professor of Physics at Guilford College in Greensboro, North Carolina. His research interests involve transient sources of light in the sky, including material falling into black holes and the death throes of giant stars. He has helped to build and used space-based X-ray telescopes as well as robotic optical telescopes on mountains around the world. He finds it wondrous to live in a time when human observations and creativity have constructed a powerful story that explains how the universe came to be the way it is and raises many more interesting questions to ponder.

SEEKING MEANING IN CREATION

Don Smith

A Quaker Astrophysicist

I am a Quaker and a scientist. To my way of thinking, these descriptions of my identity are complementary and interwoven. They have been part of me for a long time. As a scientist, I seek to discover an accurate description of the workings of the physical world I inhabit. I specialized in astrophysics because I was captivated by the beauty of the sky. I have always wanted to know more about what is out there and how it got that way. As a Quaker, I seek to find a deeper vision for the spiritual world that nurtures my being. These quests are not mutually exclusive, nor are they identical, but I think I am both a scientist and a Quaker because I have found similar tools to be useful along each path.

In this chapter I will explain how these aspects of my identity inform my reading of creation stories, particularly the creation stories in the Bible. I will look at how physicists have developed a narrative that explains the history of the universe to date. I will present my understanding of biblical creation stories in the context of this narrative, and I will explain the importance of contradiction to my search for knowledge.

Both the scientific method and Quaker spiritual traditions are rooted in skepticism. Quakers recognized early on that not every feeling they had was inspired by

3

God. When Quakers feel a spiritual leading, we are called to test it, to compare our conclusions with our traditions and the perspectives of other Friends. We must be prepared to cast aside even our most dearly held beliefs if they do not pass these tests. Quaker business meetings could not function if Friends did not enter them with the good will to listen. Without that good will, a member of the meeting could attempt to hold the sense of the meeting hostage to his or her individual perspective, demanding that consensus be achieved by bowing to his or her will. Faithful process demands we share our concerns humbly and that we listen to others with open minds.

Science, too, places high demands on those who follow its procedures. Every claim must be tested against available evidence. Regardless of how desperately we long for a favored idea to be true, we are compelled to abandon it, if the evidence so demands. The scientific profession's greatest scorn is reserved not for those who advance mistaken hypotheses (we know we all make mistakes), but for those who cling to ideas that experiment has disproved. In fact, those who think carefully about science realize that science can never establish what *is* true, it can only rule out that which is false. If we're being careful when we describe a well-established theory, scientists prefer to say that it's "not wrong" rather than that it's right.

Both science and Quakerism recognize that the truths we know are merely descriptions of reality and not reality itself. I find the Quaker practice of using queries to express our faith shifts the spiritual focus away from affirming a particular set of words toward the goal of seeking a better understanding. This is not to say that no ultimate Truths can be found, only that trying to lock Truth into particular words is a dangerous undertaking. Words are descriptions—approximations of aspects of reality that they attempt to encapsulate. Their usefulness is wholly dependent on context: we construct what we think they mean via a dynamic interaction of context and background. Since culture changes, and people age, the same set of words will not always mean the same thing. For example, George Fox said "this I know experimentally," but to a modern audience, "this I know experientially" would be closer to his meaning. It is ultimately futile to confuse words with absolute truths.

Quakers are also like scientists when we emphasize speaking from our experience. Because each of us is limited in our perspective, it is not always clear how, or if, our experiences can be generalized to apply to others. Quakers can affirm the experiences themselves without specifying the conclusions to be drawn from them. Similarly, scientists know that they might not have the right underlying theory, but the data should not be discounted. The data are the foundation; the theories are the constructs we build upon them.

The stories in the Bible are a part of my spiritual foundation, and I find I cannot read the Bible as only a Quaker or only a scientist. Both these identities inform my approach to the book. My Quaker self approaches the texts in the Bible as I would messages shared in a meeting for worship—inspired by God, perhaps, but also shaped by the human vessels through which they came and therefore dependent on those persons' cultures, backgrounds, and perspectives. When I read the Bible, I feel I am participating in a meeting for worship that extends across thousands of years in time and thousands of miles in space. These authors, my fellow travelers, wrote the words they felt best encapsulated their spiritual experience, and I receive those words humbly and with great interest.

At the same time, I know that we all have limits on our perceptions, and all claims must meet the test of evidence. We use words to communicate, and we construct the meanings of those words from the associations they raise—associations that make sense at a given time within a given culture. The construction of meaning is a dynamic process; ink on a page is meaningless until connections are created in the brain of a reader. I know from speaking two languages that even simple words can take on different meanings in translation. When reading words from texts that have been copied, recopied, merged, split, translated, annotated, lost, found, and translated again, I am very careful about the conclusions I draw about meaning.

To honor those who wrote, I try to understand as best I can who they were and what they were trying to convey. At the same time, I recognize that I can only read as myself, and the shape of my mind determines how I can receive what they said. If I do not know the context, I can misunderstand their message. I remember once reading a city woman's reaction to spending a year as a shepherd. She said that after spending months struggling with stubborn, willful, stupid creatures that are always acting against their best interests, she realized that when Jesus likened us to sheep, it might not have been a compliment. I have to open myself to the possibility that my background might mislead me in my attempts to understand, and I have to be willing to bend myself to hear a foreign perspective.

What I cannot do is willfully insist that the author must have meant something completely beyond his or her cultural context in order to achieve agreement with a claim that I believe to be true. I cannot bend the author to fit my perspective. I feel compelled to read the author's words as clearly and as thoroughly as I can, and then either agree or disagree. To force those words to fit my desires feels inconsistent with the intellectual and spiritual honesty that both Quakerism and science demand.

Stories, Myths, and Contradictions

For me, the most fruitful way to examine the biblical creation stories is to describe them as myths. The word "myth" has many connotations, and in this essay I will use the word myth in a very specific and limited sense: I designate as "myth" a story about the past that is used to give meaning to the present.

A myth gives reason to the current state of things by explaining how they came to be. A myth helps direct our choices in the present moment by placing our actions in the context of an ongoing narrative. A myth can be personal, as when an autobiography explains how someone came to be where and who she is. A myth can be national, as when Americans shape their political discourse by describing what they think the Founding Fathers intended. A myth can be spiritual, as when human suffering is explained by a fall from grace.

For most of human history, the stories that described the creation of the universe lay firmly in the territory of religion. Less than a century ago science could not provide a useful myth. Science is rooted in observation, a process that reveals much about the present but can only peer into the past with great difficulty. Since light travels at a constant but finite speed, it follows that light from distant sources must be older than light from nearby sources. Since the intensity of light diminishes as the distance to its source increases, if we wish to examine the very distant past we must look at the faintest sources of light. It was not until the 1920s that technology enhanced our eyesight enough for us to be able to measure the history of the universe. Astronomers and physicists have spent the eighty years since then using observations of light from space to construct such a history, which we call the Big Bang Theory.

This theory is the most accurate story we have of the history of the universe. I chose the word "accurate" deliberately. I believe it would be helpful if we all got used to thinking of our descriptions of the world as "accurate" or "useful" rather than "true." It is easier to discard less accurate theories as more accurate ones become available, but we become emotionally invested in what we think is true. What we accept as true becomes woven into our sense of identity, and therefore a threat to it becomes a threat to ourselves. We cease to think rationally about the evidence and lash out at that which threatens us. It is well known that human brains exhibit a "confirmation bias": we tend to devalue or ignore that which is inconsistent with what we already believe to be true. It is easier to take note of that which confirms what we believe.

The most important tool we have for shaping our myths is contradiction. Contradiction serves at least two purposes. First and most obviously, it lets us reject bad theories. Confirmation of a theory's predictions does not necessarily prove a theory is true, but we can confidently say that a theory whose predictions do not match observation is false. This process of improving useful theories and discarding false ones is how science provides an increasingly accurate description of the universe. Second, contradiction can play a more complex role than simply deciding between acceptance and rejection. A contradiction in perspectives can lead to a deeper and more subtle understanding of the issue at question.

For example, physics at the moment finds itself in the remarkable position of having two wildly successful theories that cannot both be true as we currently understand them. Einstein's famous theory of General Relativity provides a description of gravity based on the premise that what we experience as a gravitational force can be modeled as a warping of time and space. The more mass or energy there is in a given location, the more warped the space-time and the stronger the gravitational force around that location will be. A common metaphor for this description of gravity is that of a bowling ball on a trampoline: the weight of the ball curves the trampoline, and the curvature of the trampoline determines how a handful of marbles will roll around the bowling ball. General Relativity demands that space be smoothly curved, like the trampoline. The heavier the bowling ball, the more energy it has, the more strongly curved the trampoline becomes, and vice versa: the more curved the trampoline, the more energy has to be there to curve it. A sharp kink or discrete jump in space would demand an infinite amount of energy.

On the other hand, Quantum Mechanics, the physical description of how the universe behaves on the scales of subatomic particles, describes space as a "foam" of highly turbulent, violent, fluctuations. According to this description, on the smallest scales (smaller than we have been able to actually measure), space is anything *but* smooth. And, the smaller you look, the sharper and more violent the fluctuations. General relativity demands an infinite amount of energy to make these fluctuations. Both General Relativity and Quantum Mechanics cannot be right. The universe cannot be both smooth and turbulent, and yet both theories have passed every experimental test yet devised.

In the past, this kind of contradiction has led to a more comprehensive theory that uses a new conceptualization of the universe to show that each of the conflicting theories are just approximations of the truth, and do not encompass the whole picture. Contradictions between electricity and magnetism in the nineteenth century led to the understanding that both phenomena are different manifestations of the same force. The bits that make up atoms were thought of as particles (in one spot, like a grain of sand) until they were observed to act like waves (which are not confined to one spot: they stretch down an entire beach), a contradiction pointing to the deeper conceptualizations of matter explored in Quantum

Mechanics in the early twentieth century. Physicists today hope that the contradiction between General Relativity and Quantum Mechanics will yield a deeper understanding of the universe in the twenty-first century. By looking carefully at contradictions, we can refine the stories we tell and make more accurate myths.

A Scientific Myth

The main tool of science, the ability to test and discard theories, has enabled humans to construct stories about our origins that can be tested against available data. As a scientist, I have come to be convinced that the Big Bang Theory represents (for now) the most accurate story available. This story forms the backdrop against which I must read the biblical creation stories, so I will explain it briefly here.

The most recent data from observations of the most distant observable parts of the universe indicate that the universe was very hot and dense about 13.7 billion years ago, and has been expanding and cooling ever since. There are four main lines of evidence to support this scenario. First of all, we observe that light from distant galaxies has been stretched. In fact, the further away from us these galaxies are, the more their light has been stretched. This would indicate that the space of the universe is expanding. If that is the case, we can imagine "running the movie backwards," which would bring everything in the universe closer together.

The closer the elements of the universe get, the more often they will collide with each other, and the more violent those collisions will be. Eventually, molecules will break into atoms. Go further back, and atoms will shatter. Go back beyond that, and nuclei themselves will break apart into protons and neutrons. Earlier still, only quarks can survive the relentless battering. Here is where physics must stop. We do not yet have a theory, let alone data, for how (or if) quarks break into smaller pieces. This, roughly 10^{-35} seconds (about one trillionth of one trillionth of one trillionth of one second) after "the beginning" is as far back as the Big Bang Theory can go.

From that starting point, the Big Bang Theory tells a story of how the universe has been expanding and cooling for the last fourteen billion years. This story leads to four independent predictions that demand four different techniques to test four completely different data sets (which probe four different spans of time in the history of the universe). All four come up with the same answer. The way the universe expands, the amount of Hydrogen, Helium and Lithium in the universe, the characteristics of the Cosmic Microwave Background Radiation, and the large-scale clustering of galaxies are all consistent with what the Big Bang predicts.[1]

This confluence of four predictions is a remarkable success and explains why the Big Bang Theory has become the standard cosmology to professional astronomers. We believe it is the most accurate description that humans have yet constructed of the history of the universe. It is a story that explains how the universe came to be the way it is today. If it is accurate, it predicts that the universe will

---

[1] For a clear and readable treatment of the Big Bang scenario, I recommend Fred Adams' *The Living Multiverse*.

continue to expand into the future, until all the stars burn out, galaxies dissolve, and black holes evaporate. It will take more than 10^{150} years,[2] but eventually there will be nothing left.

The Big Bang Theory is a story that explains how the universe came to be the way we observe it today and projects a description of how it will continue to develop into the future. It is a story that begins in the fire of fusion and unravels into the dead-cold of ever-increasing separations. For the story to fulfill the role of myth, it must grant meaning, and I struggle to find my place within its grandeur. It is not a story that puts one race, or even one planet, as the end goal of an intentional process. The Earth is a tiny, tiny mote that formed as a by-product and has absolutely no impact on the possible outcomes. How can we find meaning in this vast irrelevance?

To me, when I think about the future stretching forward into the infinite dark, the present becomes all the more precious. Physical immortality, even if only in terms of what we might build to leave behind us after we die, is ultimately an illusion. Eventually, even atoms will vanish. The present moment is a gift, to be treasured and nurtured. It is difficult to come to terms with such vast

---

[2] 10^{150} is an almost unimaginably huge number. It is a one with one hundred and fifty zeros after it. It is more than a trillion times a trillion times a trillion times a trillion times a trillion times a trillion times a trillion times a trillion times a trillion times a trillion times a trillion.
10^{150} years is a really, really, really long time.

numbers, but the facts of the universe seem to demand this story.

Biblical Stories of Creation

The collection of texts we call "the Bible" provides other stories that try to make sense of the universe. These stories have a basis very different from the Big Bang Theory, but they share with it the desire to explain why things are the way they are. It is important to recognize both the similarities and differences between these mythic structures. The creation stories in Genesis are not scientific theories: they do not pose testable hypotheses nor do they attempt to include all possible data in their scenarios.

They are also not poetic expressions of the Big Bang. Some people try to find verses that seem like metaphors for modern understandings, but this effort is flawed, methodologically and theologically. By selecting the parts that fit our preconceptions and ignoring those that don't, we are highly vulnerable to confirmation bias; we can make *any* random set of data support *any* claim with that procedure.

Furthermore, by focusing in on single words or phrases, our interpretation is highly sensitive to translation issues. From a theological perspective, it seems egocentric in the extreme to think that God would hide messages only understandable to scientifically literate people of the 21st century in a text that is supposed to be for all humanity throughout time. I do not believe that God, who presumably does know the true history of the universe, spoon-fed an encoded version of the truth to the ancient writers.

I cannot look at the texts in this way. I believe that the ancient authors were trying to express their own faith, within their own understanding and their own cultural context, and this is the perspective from which I approach their writings. My goal as I approach Genesis is not to prove or disprove the correctness of the stories it tells. I do not want to stretch their message to fit my understanding; to claim we are really saying the same thing. I want to appreciate their stories and discover what they can say to me.

As a basis for approaching the text, I am convinced of the accuracy of the scholarly consensus that different pieces of Genesis were written by different authors at different times and that their work was woven together by a skillful editor at some later date. Even in English translation, one can tell that different parts of the book have different styles, vocabularies, and theologies. Sometimes the sections by different authors follow each other, and sometimes they are woven tightly together, sentence by sentence.

In the first two chapters of Genesis, we have two stories, placed back to back, of how the world came to be. The first chapter paints its story on a cosmic scale. Light is created, the heavens are separated from the earth, and all manner of plants and animals are brought into being. The second chapter brings the story down to an intimate level by examining the creation of humanity and how people were placed in the Garden of Eden, to till and tend it.

In the second chapter (actually written centuries earlier than the first), God is highly anthropomorphized. He has breath, walks in the Garden, and has to ask questions to find out what the people have been up to. The author of Chapter 1 has a grander vision and rejects this conception of God in favor of a more cosmic creator—distant, powerful, and in control. Still more centuries later, we catch a glimpse of yet another vision of creation, in the first few lines of the Gospel of John. Here we are presented with a complex relationship between God and God's "Word" (in Greek, *logos*), which are somehow both the same and yet separate.

The differences between these stories are part of the evidence that has convinced me that the Bible as we know it was not born from one single vision but encapsulates a sprawling and ongoing conversation about the human race, God, creation, and our role in it.

A Cosmic Creator

The first chapter of Genesis opens with a grand vision: God creates light to shine into the darkness of the waters of primordial chaos. The deity then divides these waters to create a safe space between the waters above the sky and the waters of the sea. The creation of the world is thereby an affirmation of order: a simple assertion of control.

Karen Armstrong claims that this account of creation is also a response to the Babylonian creation myth, in which Marduk (male God of war) creates the world through battle with the beast Tiamat, goddess of chaos. Her body is cloven to create the division between earth and sky. The world born of this conflict is dangerous, precarious, and hostile.

Genesis 1 rejects the Babylonian myth. In Genesis, the world is created intentionally, "and it was good." There was no colossal battle with the force of chaos: God spoke, and the chaos parted. Instead of associating sea monsters with powerful gods of chaos, on a similar level with the Creator but defeated by him, those monsters are simply stuck into a list of created beings, subject to God's authority like everything else. Neither are the sun and moon described as gods; they are also created objects. This perspective has become so ingrained in our culture that it is difficult to imagine how radical it must have been when it was written.

The author of Genesis 1 is even more radical when it comes to human beings. He or she does not associate maleness with good and femaleness with evil, as in the Marduk/Tiamat story. Humans are created male and female at the same time, and both are affirmed as good. In fact, the author goes further to claim that humans are made in God's image. After the cosmic majesty of what God has created so far, to be made in God's image is a remarkable vision of human potential. It is this vision that led J.R.R. Tolkien to conclude that the highest goal to which a human can aspire is to create something, for in so doing we are acting in the image of our Creator.

It is interesting, as a modern scientist, to note that the text does not demand creation *ex nihilo*. The primordial chaos was there. God made the ordered universe out of it, but there is no explanation of where the chaos came from. The text also does not explain the origin of the audience for God's comment "let us make man in our image," nor does it try to explain the origin of God himself. Unlike the Greek or Norse gods, this deity comes from nowhere, and has no siblings or parents. The story starts with the creation of light. What was before that? This story does not try to say. In that sense, the author was not too dissimilar from modern cosmologists, who describe how the universe evolved from the chaotic soup of densely packed subatomic particles, but cannot yet say where those particles came from. It is a fallacy to conclude that because physics cannot explain the origin of the universe, there must be a designer behind it. Who designed the designer? Even the Bible does not try to address this question.

As an astronomer reading Chapter 1, it startles me most that the sun and moon were created on the fourth day. For the first three days, there was evening and there was morning: another day had passed, but without the sun and moon. Cause and effect are reversed: the sun is put in the sky during the day because it is day. Day is not caused by the sun being above the horizon. This would seem to imply that the author does not associate night and day with the presence of the sun in the sky. The text states that the sun and moon are put there to be signs for the seasons, which is, of course, how astronomy got its start: as a means to track planting and harvesting times. On the other hand, the text does say one purpose of the sun and moon is "to give light upon the Earth," so I am not clear whether the author really sees night and day as separate from the sun and moon or whether the idea is just a storytelling device.

In either case, it is clear to me that the pattern of the story demands we reject the idea that the "days" in this chapter could be metaphors for the vast eras of time that the modern scientific theory demands. It has been argued that since the sun and moon were not yet created, the first three days could have actually lasted billions of what we now call years. I have even heard it said that the Hebrew word translated "day" here does not necessarily have to refer to a rigid twenty-four-hour interval. My knowledge of Hebrew is insufficient to substantiate this claim, but it seems to me to clearly work against the intentions of the author.

The whole chapter follows the pattern "there was evening, there was morning," which heralds a new day. The sun and moon are put in place on the third day, precisely to mark the separation of day from night. There is no internal indication in the text that the fifth day is any different in length from the second. There is no hint that the author intended the days to be anything other than literal twenty-four hour days. To impose that interpretation on the text to make it conform to what we now think to be true does not seem fair to the spirit of what that author was trying to say three thousand years ago.

What I hear coming through the text is that the author had a grand vision of how the deity related to his creation, and he or she wrote with passion and conviction. The Creator of the world did not struggle with a nearly equal enemy, for God had no equals. The creation was not flawed and dangerous, but good in every respect. God spoke, and order was formed from chaos over six (equal) days. Just because the author was not writing a scientific story, it does not seem fair to distort what he or she was trying to say. Ironically, that is exactly what happens when the cosmic creator deity is paired with the limited, human-like God we meet in Chapter 2.

A Limited God

Chapter 2 of Genesis (technically, the first few verses of Chapter 2 finish up the narrative of the Chapter 1 story — the Chapter 2 story doesn't start until verse 5) does not present us with an origin story for the Earth as a whole. This chapter focuses almost exclusively on the creation of a human couple. Although plants and animals are created as well, they are explicitly created for and around the human. The Earth is already there, a lifeless and dusty place, and the deity, here called Yahweh, starts by making a man out of the dust. Chapter 2 is much more detailed and specific than Chapter 1. Chapter 1 gives no details as to *how* God created these things: God spoke, and it was so. The only suggestion that it took any effort was that God had to rest at the end of it. The Yahweh story in contrast is full of detail: Yahweh shapes Adam from dust, breathes into Adam's nostrils, and plants the Garden of Eden.

Perhaps the story we read in Chapter 2 had a first chapter as well, which the later editor did not preserve, in favor of the Chapter 1 we now have. I find it interesting to speculate about what the original Chapter 1 might have looked like. Without the grand, cosmic vision of the later author, perhaps the Yahweh creation story was more similar to the Babylonian stories. Perhaps the scattered fragmentary references to stories of Yahweh defeating serpents (Isaiah 27:1, Job 26:13, Psalm 74:13) are relics of a lost Hebrew version of the Babylonian myth that might have preceded Chapter 2. Who knows, perhaps the first chapter of Genesis was written with the express purpose of directly contradicting the lost first chapter of the Yahweh story.

Ultimately, it's not possible to be certain whether or not a story of Yahweh creating the Earth ever existed. As a physicist, this level of uncertainty is both frustrating and reassuring to me. Frustrating because short of finding a lost text, there is no experiment we can perform and no number we can compute that will allow us to reject either hypothesis. We must try to decide what scenario is most likely, an endeavor fraught with difficulty, since what each of us feels is "most likely" will depend on our experiences of how the world tends to work. In so far as we have shared experiences, we will tend to agree on what is most likely.

On the other hand, as long as there is uncertainty, there is room for learning and discovery, and hence uncertainty is at the core of what science is and who scientists are. We rule out bad models, but even our best models are uncertain. When we are certain we have all the answers, we stop asking questions, and then we cannot recognize the opportunities the universe generously grants us to push ourselves to the next level.

It is most unfortunate that the twentieth century put forward scientists as a kind of priesthood for dispensing truths. It seems to me that "science has shown" became a secular version of "the Bible says," as if science ends discussions rather than starting them. This substitution misses the joy that comes with not knowing the answer and sets people up for disillusionment when scientists (as they inevitably will) come up with a better theory. We may never know whether the author of Chapter 2 wrote an earlier creation story, so we must come to terms with uncertainty, which is another way that science and religion converge, in my perspective.

Whether there was a lost first chapter or no, it seems clear that the editor who merged these two stories added a phrase or two to make the text flow better. He also makes it look like the Chapter 2 story was simply going back and looking in more detail at what happened on the third day. The joining is hardly seamless, because in addition to the stylistic and conceptual differences discussed above, these two stories order the creation of humans, plants and animals quite differently.

The Chapter 2 narrative describes how Yahweh creates Adam from the dust in the (as yet) plantless ground, then creates plants for him to eat and till. Later still, in the somewhat bizarre quest to find Adam "a helper and partner," Yahweh tries creating every animal on the planet as a potential mate for Adam. Although Adam names all the animals, the quest fails and Yahweh finally brings Eve forth from the rib of the sleeping Adam.

This version of events is completely different from that of Chapter 1, where the sequence of creation begins with plants, continues with animals, and culminates in humanity. Here, a man is created first, then plants, then animals, and finally, a woman. The first chapter does not specify that only one couple is made, but the second chapter does, leading to the startling revelation that when Adam and Eve's son Cain is exiled after killing his brother, he goes to live with people in the land of Nod. Where did they come from?

The details of this story are so familiar, it is hard to see them with fresh eyes and recognize how foreign the worldview of the author really is from that of the author of Chapter 1, let alone that of a person living in the twenty-first-century. How can we, who are used to the idea that God is omniscient and omnipotent, make sense of a God who doesn't know that Adam would need a human female as a partner? I keep wanting to think it's just a game Yahweh is playing, but the text is quite explicit about Yahweh's motives. This is a very foreign God!

On the other hand, there is something comforting in a God who is not wholly removed from human experience. There's something appealing about a God who digs into the dust and gets his hands dirty. As an astrophysicist who tries to study the vastness of creation, I tend to lean toward a God who is also vast and timeless. It is good for me to have alternate stories like this one to make me think about a more limited God, who might be more accessible to a tiny little biped on a rock spinning through space.

The Word

The description of creation at the start of the Gospel of John is in many ways the hardest story for me to make sense of, in part because of its brevity.

In the beginning was the word, and the word was with God, and the word was God. He was in the beginning with God. (John 1:1)

Scholars assure me that "the word" or *logos* (in Greek) is an allusion to the concept of God's creative and reasoning power, an idea borrowed from Greek philosophy. I am also reminded of the (much later) idea from Jewish Cabbalistic theology that the act of creation involved a sundering of the Divinity into fragments, the reunification of which is the goal of the instructions of the Torah.

The writer of the Gospel of John takes the idea of a multi-faceted deity in a different direction than the Cabbalists, saying Jesus in this world was a manifestation of the very creative force through which God caused the world to come into being. It is easy to think of this story as describing the events in Genesis 1, and connect "the word" with the actual words given there: "let there be light." Surely, the author of John is simply describing the events in Genesis 1.

This simple answer does not ring true to me. At the very least, it seems clear to me that these two authors had different processes in mind. The *logos* of John seems to allude to more than just the declarations of God in Genesis 1, and Genesis 1 in no way gives the spoken words of God any kind of identity as a being or aspect. Although the deity of Chapter 1 is far less anthropomorphic than the Yahweh we meet in Chapter 2, there is no hint that the pronouncements are to be taken as any more than statements of intent. And yet, when God says "let there be light," there is light. Perhaps the Johannine passage is an attempt to suggest *how* God's proclamations lead to alterations of reality.

The most fascinating difference between the Johannine story and the stories in Genesis is that the gospel's author is specific and explicit about the meaning he wishes to convey about the creation story. If a myth is a story that gives meaning to why we are here, the Genesis chapters are more open to interpretation. You can argue about what it means to be created "good," or whether Eve's later creation has implications for gender relations, but the gospel's author explicitly ties his creation story to the ironic message of his overall narrative: God came into his creation, and that creation "knew him not."

The author develops this ironic theme of not recognizing our savior/creator throughout his gospel, but right here in the first sentence he starts on the grandest scale possible: he ties Jesus' story, and our relation to it, to the story of the creation of the universe. Therefore, it is a story that matters in the strongest possible terms. He makes Jesus' life story into a myth by casting Jesus as the creator and pointing out that we are his creation. That connection raises each of us and our choices out of insignificance.

The Importance of Contradiction

These three stories are rife with contradiction. From trivial facts about the order of creation to huge questions about the nature and scope of God's power, these authors do not agree. As a scientist reading these texts, I must therefore come to terms with contradiction.

I find it sad when people either cannot admit that the contradictions are there or use the contradictions as an excuse to throw out the whole endeavor. These texts were written by people with different viewpoints. Putting them in the same book introduces a creative tension that has spawned millennia of thought and argument. The Bible, if taken as a single whole, presents a god who is *both* cosmic *and* personal, both single and multi-faceted. We read of a god who created the universe but who can still be wrestled down by Jacob.

From my point of view, contradictions are not "gotchas" that reveal the humbug behind the curtain in Oz. They are lights that illuminate an object from different angles: one reveals what the other left in shadow. By comparing and contrasting a diverse collection of perspectives we gain a richer understanding of what each person is trying to say and how we ourselves react to them. Quakers do not expect everyone in a meeting for worship to share the same viewpoint. We believe that as more of us share our perspectives, our community will come closer to the truth than any of us would on our own.

If all we had was one side of the story, it would not challenge us to think; we could simply accept or reject it. A Quaker teenager once told me he enjoyed his school debate club because of how contrast reveals meaning. He learned that if someone says "this chair is green," and you agree, then you both nod and go on your way. If, however, you say "no, the chair is blue," then you have to confront just what it is that you mean. You have to explore what color is, what green and blue are, and perhaps even what a chair is. In the end you understand better just what it is you believe, even if those beliefs are unchanged by the examination.

If there were only one biblical story and that story already matched our preconceptions, we would simply accept that our interpretation was the one natural meaning of the text. The idea of an all-powerful God is so ingrained in our culture it has become self-evident to us now. We would not realize how radical this idea was at the time

Chapter 1 was written if we did not have the second chapter's older vision of a limited Yahweh to contrast with it. The first chapter of John pushes us to think about just what the words of God are and how creation was accomplished. The Big Bang reminds us that the universe is vaster than anything those authors could have dreamed and keeps us humble about what we think we know. Multiple, conflicting viewpoints jolt us out of complacency and force us to examine our beliefs.

Conclusions

The biblical creation stories are not scientific theories that can be tested and disproved. They are myths that connect us to the past as we try to make sense of our lives. The Big Bang Theory provides an accurate description (as far as we can tell from the available data) of how the universe got to be the way it is now. It describes the past, but it ascribes no meaning to the story. We tell our own stories to create meaning. When people stand in a Quaker meeting to share a message, they are using their past to shed light on the present, which in turn directs us toward the future. When I read scripture, I feel that I am partaking in a meeting for worship with believers vastly different from myself. The stories they tell enrich and inform me, but ultimately I must grapple with the meaning of God myself.

As a Quaker and a scientist, I seek to embrace uncertainty and test my ideas. I try not to mistake my description of reality for the reality I describe, and I hope to listen to all who cross my path. If there was a creator who set the awesome grandeur of the Big Bang in motion, then the cosmic creator described by the author of Genesis 1 resonates strongly with my appreciation for the vastness of the cosmos. If that god has a personal connection with me, I value the vision of the author of Chapter 2 that allows Yahweh to make mistakes and fumble through as best he can. The brevity of the gospel of John points to answers and stories that lie outside the covers of one book. Ultimately, I find the presence of conflicting stories to be freeing, as I am not constrained to merely accept or reject a single story or meaning: I can construct my own myth from the data available to me, while remaining cognizant of the fact that my perspective is inherently limited. As a scientist, I am continually reminded of my limited understanding of the universe.

The common thread between physics and the biblical stories is contradiction. Quantum Mechanics and General Relativity cannot both be true, but their contradiction points us toward a deeper understanding we have yet to achieve. Likewise the truth about God is most likely something different from either the cosmic deity or the human-like Yahweh we meet in the first chapters of Genesis. Each of these visions on their own, however, yields insight into different aspects of reality. Through exploring these different viewpoints we gain a deeper understanding of our world and our role in it, while remaining mindful that there is so much more to figure out. What an exciting prospect!

Bibliography

Armstrong, Karen. *In the Beginning*. New York: Ballantine Books, 1996

Adams, Fred. *Our Living Multiverse*. New York: Pi Press, 2004.

Barbour, Ian. *When Science Meets Religion*. New York: HarperCollins, 2000.

Friedman, Richard. *Who Wrote the Bible*. New York: Simon & Schuster, 1987.

Gamov, George. *Mr. Tompkins in Wonderland*. Cambridge: Cambridge University Press, 1940.

Greene, Brian. *The Elegant Universe*. New York: W. W. Norton & Co., 1999.

Tolkien, J.R.R. *The Monsters & the Critics*. London: HarperCollins, 1990.

Anthony Prete is a member of Central Philadelphia Monthly Meeting, which supports his ministry of bringing the fruits of progressive biblical scholarship to unprogrammed Friends. Tony has carried out this ministry by teaching at Adult First Day Schools, and at Pendle Hill in conjunction with the Resident Student Program. He has conducted numerous workshops at FGC Gatherings; his 2003 plenary address, "Shalom: Much More Than Just Peace," also appeared in *Friends Journal* (Nov. 2003). He has eight course offerings in the Philadelphia Yearly Meeting's traveling teachers list. His biblical articles and book reviews appear in *Friends Journal*.

Tony has pursued graduate biblical studies at La Salle University and the Lutheran Theological Seminary in Philadelphia. His teaching emphasizes the richness of the original biblical languages and literary forms, especially in Psalms and Genesis. He lives in Haddonfield New Jersey with his wife Trish, who is an attender at Central Philadelphia.

A GOD OF SURPRISES

Anthony Prete

Creation (Genesis 1:1-2:4)

Something inside me clicked into place when I learned that the seven-day creation account took shape during or after the Babylonian Exile (587-538 B.C.E.). Of course! What else would you do after a conquering army had laid siege to your city, savagely killed your people or drove them into exile, and reduced to rubble the temple where you communed with your God? What else would you do when this God—the one who had promised to protect you—did not lift a finger as the Babylonian forces swept over you like a sand storm? What else would you do when you could not shake the question: Had our God, the one we believed was the most powerful of all the gods, been overwhelmed and defeated by Marduk, the god of the Babylonians?

Wracked by such questions, the Israelites faced a defining choice. They could give up on their God and look for another—Marduk, perhaps—who would protect them in exchange for their worship and allegiance. Or they could, without a shred of evidence supporting it and with overwhelming evidence refuting it, reaffirm their faith in the God of their ancestors. The Israelites chose the latter, and one form that their choice took is the creation account in Genesis 1:1-2:4. This poem affirms their God as the power and the genius that called into existence, part by part, the entire world as they knew it. What a leap: from a God who apparently failed them and wandered off, wounded and powerless, to a God at whose word all of creation sprang into existence and functioned as this God directed.

Had I not known this exilic background—which the text presumes but does not reveal—I would not have recognized this text as a bold and defiant manifesto by a defeated and dislocated people. I learned further that they built their case by taking what the science of their time understood about the world, and positioning their God at each stage as the one who calls it forth, assigns its function, affirms its goodness. They used their captors' own creation story, the *Enuma Elish*. But that story posits violence among the gods as the source of creation; the Israelites' God creates by words of invitation—the very antithesis of violence. How could I not look more closely, listen more deeply, investigate more thoroughly this courageous expression of faith.

Once I was able to see the Babylonian Exile as the driving force, and other ancient myths as the backtext to the biblical creation story, I started to wonder what else I might be missing. I needed to listen for a better grasp of what God was saying to the defeated and disillusioned Israelites back in the sixth century B.C.E.—whether through stories that passed from one generation to the next, or through sophisticated poetry that makes up much of what they wrote.

Confirmation and Conflict

What I heard brought both confirmation and conflict. Yes, acknowledging the awesomeness of this Creator God who conquers chaos and establishes protective boundaries helped put the faith of the Israelites (and my own faith) back on track. The calmness of the story evokes a confidence, not just in the God who made the world but in the world that this God made. At each stage, God declares it "good"—not potentially good or good if it works out, but good in and of itself. Even the poem's folkloric simplicity, with light created on Day One (Genesis 1:3-5) and the sun and moon on Day Four (1:14-19),[1] reinforced the authenticity of its experiential tones.

But as I took in the text something about it rang hollow. The world it describes clashed with what I know today—not just physically but functionally. What I was reading seemed more like somebody's fantasy, a world wished into being. In the world we know today, chaos continues to surface and boundaries are regularly breached.

Then I began to wonder: If the earth as I see it today appears to contradict the creation story, how much more so would it have seemed to the victims of Babylonian military might. Indeed, their world was the polar opposite of what the first creation account so glowingly describes. Even worse, the very majesty of the Creator God was, in their eyes, brought low by Babylonian defeat and destruction. Perhaps, then, the gap between what the text

---

[1] Unless otherwise indicated, all citations are from Genesis. All translations are from the New Revised Standard Version.

says and what the Israelites (and I) experienced is intentional. The creation account was the world as God intended it; current events were the world as it had become.

If the gap between ancient text and contemporary experience exists, the Israelites, rising above defeat and exile, bridged it with their trust in God's faithfulness. The creation story was the *first* word about their God, not the last. Nor did it represent some enduring idyllic state. In fact, hardly is the story told than it starts to crumble; by chapter six (as we will see in the second part of this essay), it will totter on the edge of the chaos it originally overcame.

Reading as a Quaker

As Quakers, we place great emphasis on listening to the Inner Teacher. We trust that we are Spirit-guided, and this guidance is our ultimate criterion for determining whether or not a particular idea is "of God." When we read the Bible, we seek to determine what God is saying to us through the text. And it is certainly possible that as we hover over that text we will hear God's voice. It may speak to us of a decision we're struggling to make, a problem we're seeking to resolve, or an obstacle we're striving to overcome. It may open us to a new awareness of God's presence, of the beauty in the world around us, of our oneness with all creation.

Or it may not. The passage may only puzzle us, or even anger us. Depending on where in the Bible we are reading, we may find that it does not "speak to our condition" at all—or at least, so it may seem. There are logical reasons for this. To read the Bible is to enter into a strange society and an ancient time, to encounter peculiar and often disturbing customs, sometimes to find ourselves repelled by what we read. What then? Do we dismiss the text, moving on to somewhere else—perhaps another part of the Bible, perhaps another inspirational book, perhaps even another spiritual tradition?

Many Friends have done just that, and not without justification; the Bible is no easy book to read. In fact, it is not even a book. It is a collection of books, containing material that originated in various ancient times, was written in various strange styles, and compiled by various unknown people. It is nothing like any contemporary volume that we would read; appearances notwithstanding, it does not proceed smoothly from beginning to middle to end. What's more, it lacks factual verification and is repetitious and sometimes even self-contradictory. The Bible is hardly a book to scan or read quickly, as one might a novel or a news story. In short, it is a problematic read.

I maintain that such problems cannot be resolved simply by listening to our Inner Teacher. I say that, not because I doubt God's ability to enlighten us, but because I am convinced that we are not the only ones hearing God's voice. So, I seek out those others and listen to what they say. As scholars, they have scrutinized the text with skills and sensitivities that I do not possess, and have come up with insights, explanations and conclusions that are otherwise beyond my reach.

Searching the Scholars

In my broader search for understanding and insight, I relied on biblical scholars who could lead me through this unfamiliar terrain, pointing out a feature here, a landmark there, the ruin where a house once stood, the faint trail of what used to be a major road. I learned from women and from men. I learned from Christians of various faith traditions, and from medieval rabbis and contemporary Jews. I learned from those whose scholarship focused on linguistics or archaeology. More than anything, I sought those who let the biblical text speak for itself, who struggled with difficult passages without accepting pat answers or curt dismissals, who knew the Bible so well that they could extract and articulate its foundational themes and its core convictions. The only scholars I avoided were the ones who brought an obvious agenda to their analysis of the biblical text—especially an agenda that saw Christianity as the key that unlocks the Hebrew Scriptures. I preferred those whose agendas (for we all have them) were rooted in the text.

Eventually I formed a collection of favorites, and the chief among them is Walter Brueggemann, professor emeritus at Columbia Theological Seminary in Decatur, Georgia. Brueggemann is a prolific biblical scholar and a concerned believer who refuses to leave the text resting safely in the past. Instead he uses it to engage and critique the present, writing with a clarity and precision that are faithful to the text and the times. He became my touchstone, his writings pointing me to other scholars who share his passion and his skill.

It was Brueggemann, for example, who opened me to a new and richer understanding of the flood narrative by turning my attention away from a punitive interpretation. He also helped me see that the narrative draws power from what precedes it in the text, so that's where I'd like to turn.

The Flood (Genesis 6:5-9:17)

Most readers of Genesis recognize that the first eleven chapters have an identity distinct from the rest of the book. From chapter twelve onward, the text deals with the origins of the Israelite people. Though these chapters are not history in any modern sense of the term, they do have a certain historical air. The first eleven chapters, on the other hand, lack any historical footing; in fact they precisely avoid any sense that the events they describe can be pinned to a specific time or place. Biblical commentaries refer to them as "primordial," and note similarities between them and the "stories of origins" in other ancient Near-Eastern cultures.

The Antediluvian Age

Though the primordial narratives of Genesis have no historical footing, they definitely tell a progressive story. It begins with a creation that is pronounced "good" many times, and ultimately "very good" (1:31). But from that point on, creation begins to unravel. God's gift of a garden is rejected when the craftiest of God's creatures entices the first humans to violate the one directive they had received. The divine disappointment is expressed in cursing the serpent and the earth (not, please note, the man and

woman), and in expelling the humans from the garden—
though not without God first making clothing for them
(3:21).

After deceit and disobedience comes murder—a
fratricide no less (4:1-16). Angry at God's choice of Abel's
offering over his, the tiller of the soil slays his shepherd
brother. For the first time God hears, arising from that soil,
the cry of spilled human blood. Outraged, God demands
to know, "What have you done?" It is as though God
cannot believe what the soil is saying, that the divine
plan—and with it, divine contentment—can be so easily
thwarted. Yet Cain's punishment does not fit the crime;
rather than death, the soil will be his sentence. It will resist
him, making him "a fugitive and a wanderer on the earth."
Though God does not take his life, Cain fears that others
will. This idea is so repulsive to God that it evokes a divine
"Not so!" and a promise of "sevenfold vengeance" for
anyone who takes Cain's life. God then places a protective
mark on Cain—a kindness that recalls the clothes God
made for his parents.

A brief genealogy follows, ending with Lamech (4:23-
24), the veritable junkyard dog of Genesis. He boasts to his
wives that he killed someone who only wounded him, and
a young man simply for striking him. Arrogantly he
appropriates to himself the protection that God placed on
Cain—but with a seventy-fold increase. Thus Lamech
escalates deterrence to vengeance, and does it with words
that until now have been only God's to speak. God, for the
first time, says nothing.

Next, a long genealogy ties Adam to Lamech,
emphasizing the hundreds of years that each generation

lived. Following this is what appears to be an obscure textual remnant (6:1-4)—complete with rapacious "sons of God" and mysterious "Nephilim." Apparently, little is left that God can call "good." Chaos, once sent packing, has slipped back onto the scene and is sucking more and more of creation into its void.

A Question of Interpretation

We come then to the point in Genesis where divine disappointment has reached such a depth that God decides to give chaos full rein by unleashing the waters from which creation once emerged. The traditional interpretation has an angry punitive God lashing out at pervasive sin by drowning not just the sinners but "animals and creeping things and birds of the air" (6:7)—a kind of a cosmic guilt-by-association. Is that what the story really says? The answer is not so evident. The biblical text, Genesis 6:5-9:17, is dotted with contradiction, repetition, and reversals. The writing seems loose and undisciplined; extraneous details abound. Simple questions like "How many pairs of animals were taken into the ark?" and "How long did it rain?" have no single answer (compare 6:19-20 with 7:2-3; 7:4 with 7:24). Apparently more is going on here than a simple tale with a straightforward message.

Most anyone with even rudimentary biblical training (or a good study Bible) knows that the flood account is the weaving together of two stories that developed separately among the Israelites, one from earlier in their history (900-700 B.C.E.) and the other from later (700-500 B.C.E.). Much has been made of these stories, and rightly so; they represent two of the four major sources from which the

Torah (Genesis through Deuteronomy) is ultimately constructed. Each source has a cluster of characteristics. To cite but one example from the sources for the flood story, the older tradition (identified by scholars as Yahwist) tends to emphasize God's closeness, even to the point of what might seem to be excessive anthropomorphism—a God too close. The later tradition (identified as Priestly), centered on the Jerusalem Temple, tends to emphasize the great gulf between creatures and God, even to the point of what might seem to be excessive transcendence—a God too far. The artistic blending of these two accounts preserves the power of each.

When I commented earlier on the creation account in Genesis, I emphasized the influence of the Babylonian Exile on the final formation of the biblical text. The original readers of that text, still feeling the effects of Babylonian violence and destruction, would have seen the connection intuitively. But it is invisible to us without—as I hope I have demonstrated—the help of biblical scholarship. The flood narrative bears a similar lineage and invisibility. Except now, rather than an act of defiance against their conquerors, it seems to reflect the disorientation that the exiles must have felt as everything they had was swept away and they struggled to survive in this strange and alien city. What better image than a worldwide flood to express their sense that they had no earth to stand on, no high-ground refuge, no rocky crag where they could hide and regroup.

Other ancient civilizations had their version of the flood story, and Israel's storytellers dipped into this common pool. What they pulled out, though they subsequently made it their own, is strikingly similar to the Babylonian flood story, told in *The Epic of Gilgamesh*. There, the gods decide to destroy the earth for no apparent reason. But one of them, Ea, leaks the news to a human, Utnapishtim, and gives him directions for building a ship large enough to hold "all living things" (Tablet XI, line 27). Utnapishtim complies. As the rain is about to begin, he compels his family and kin, domestic and wild animals, and all the craftspeople to board the ship. After seven days the deluge is over. As the waters recede, Utnapishtim releases birds to test for dry land. Once it is safe to leave the boat, he offers a sacrifice to the gods. The overlap with the biblical account is uncanny. Or is it?

I do not know if other flood myths also resembled that of the Babylonians, but surely the similarities were not lost on the Israelites. Nor did they simply mimic the myth of their captors, they bested it. A storm of seven days now lasts for forty (or is it 150?); the cause lies not with the apparently arbitrary decision of the gods, but with creatures who refuse to be true to their Creator; the divine assurance at the end is not just a promise to remember these days but a pledge never to repeat them.

No Longer Unique

The Bible says nothing about the influence on Israel's flood story by those of other cultures. Traditionally, then, readers have assumed this story is unique, a special revelation that only the Israelites had. This impression reinforces the assumption that the Israelite religion was unique; totally different from those of their contemporaries. How easily such uniqueness lends itself to a sense of superiority, first among the Israelites and later among Jews and Christians. And how much more easily does it incline us to miss the message of this narrative by focusing our attention on its apparently most dramatic element, the flood—to the point where we still hear reports from time to time about a sighting of the actual ark, nestled somewhere on a mountaintop.

On the other hand, to know that Israel's story of the flood was just one of numerous such stories is to reinforce the idea that Israel was never meant to be totally and entirely apart from the other nations. Rather it was meant to be a model for those nations, a model of authentic creaturely existence (12:3). Of necessity then, Israel must have had something in common with other nations. We know now that it has the flood story in common; scholars who investigate archaeology, linguistics, ancient records and the like, are finding more and more of what Israel also had in common with the smaller nations that were its immediate neighbors.

I find this to be a powerful lesson for Friends. Perhaps because our numbers are small, perhaps because our mode of worship is unusual, perhaps because of our deeply held commitments to overcome societal oppression, we risk a sense of uniqueness that can only work to our detriment. The days of conflict between opposing denominations are over. The days of staying to ourselves are over. Indeed, the days of Quakers being "special" are also over. We are part of a much larger faith community and need to learn from that community—from its scholars, its prophets, its preachers, its activists, its ordinary members. And they need to learn from us. They need to learn the importance of silently waiting in God's presence, of listening, of caution regarding the dangers of ritual worship and hierarchical authority, of quiet and constant commitment to social justice and to alleviating the oppression of others, of simplicity and integrity. This will not happen if we stay in our own enclaves; if we think that ours is the only "flood story" worth preserving.

Digging for the Message

Seeing the biblical flood story in its broader societal context takes nothing away from the power of its message. But what is that message? The answer is right in the text, but I missed it because I got caught up in torrential rains and an ark-ful of survivors. There are immediate and practical ramifications for my missing the message of the flood story. They involve what I as a grandfather must soon explain to my grandson.

From before he was born, my grandson's bedroom had a Noah's Ark "theme." I didn't mind this when he was an infant, but now he's five and he's bound to start asking questions. My fear is that the answers he hears will involve an angry God punishing bad people by drowning everyone—including babies, five-year-olds, dogs, cats, turtles, and hug-worn teddy bears.

There was a time, as I said, when I might have given him a similar answer. Now, however, I can see that such an answer misses the point—it is not what the flood narrative is saying. Primarily, this is the story of a disappointed God who is grieved because creation has gone so far off course that nothing is left but to return it to its original chaos. My image is that of a potter who has plans for an exquisite bowl. She sits at the potter's wheel and centers a carefully prepared ball of clay. But as the clay revolves, it resists the gentle pressures of her hands, it will not take the shape she envisioned. Delicate edges collapse, the bowl slips off center and starts to wobble on the wheel. Eventually the frustrated potter realizes that she has no choice but to return the bowl to the original ball of clay from which she had hoped to fashion a work of art.

Why this image? Part of the answer takes us back to the framers of the flood narrative, the Israelite exiles of the sixth century B.C.E. Their long-sought possessions of land, city, and temple are now so destroyed that their world seems to have reverted to chaos. In the same manner, God's creation, at first so promising, has deteriorated to the point where its return to chaos seems inevitable.

Why this divine determination to undo what had been proclaimed, just a few chapters back, as "very good"? The Bible answers with such words as "wickedness" and "evil" (6:5), "corrupt" and "violence" (6:11). This frequently gets interpreted as rampant sin—although the Bible's three Hebrew words for "sin" are nowhere in the text. The words that are in the text clearly point to something going wrong, but that cannot be limited to individual acts of disobedience. If anything, God has shown a tolerance for such acts: Adam and Eve did not die (2:17; 3:24); Cain, though cast out, bore the mark of God's protection (4:15). The fault needs lie in something deeper, something that cuts more to the core of creation then do the individual acts by which we harm others and ourselves.

Rather what we have is creation run amok at a profound level: its refusal to be creation. At some point, the text is telling us, creation has crossed the line. The fault does not lie in weakness, but arrogance (see 6:5); not in individuals, but in "all flesh" (6:12); not just here and there, but over the entire earth (see 6:13). The divine experiment has failed, the bowl will not hold its shape, further effort is fruitless.

The Divine Response

Thus the stage is set for God to respond. The traditional interpretations of an angry God unleashing the fury of nature have support in the text: "I will blot out" (6:7), "I have determined to make an end... I am going to destroy them" (6:13). But the text in its entirety tells us differently, provided we take the time to linger over it, resisting the urge to "cut to the action" where the waters come crashing in like some primeval tsunami.

If we do linger, if we do listen, if we do let the words truly speak to us, a different message emerges. This is not just a story of divine demolition, it is a story primarily of divine disappointment. "And the Lord was sorry that he had made humankind on the earth, and it grieved him to his heart" (6:6). How can God be "sorry"? The Hebrew term makes clear that this is not a matter of *remorse*, as though God had done something wrong and needed to apologize. Rather the issue is *regret*. Things did not turn out the way God had planned—no, not "planned" but *expected* or *hoped*. Otherwise how explain the second part of the sentence, "and it grieved him to his heart"?

Two points need mentioning here. The first is that for the ancients, the heart was not considered the seat of emotions and passions as it is for us. Rather it was the place where thinking and deciding occur—functions that are deeply personal and that define who we are. Second, the Hebrew word that's translated "grieved" involves both physical and emotional pain (its noun form is used in Genesis 3:16 to characterize the pain of childbirth that Eve would experience outside the garden). And the form of this Hebrew verb resembles our reflexive tense: something one does to oneself or allows to be done to oneself. Thus God's grief, evoked by the condition of creation, arises from within, is true pain, and reaches the deepest levels of who God is.

Those words forced me to question my childhood images of a perfect God who sees all and knows all, who does everything exactly right, and who could never ever make a mistake or be disappointed. The text is unequivocal: "regretted," "grieved."

This is not far-fetched. Undergirding the biblical narrative is a quest by the Israelites to discern the actions of God in their everyday life, then use that discernment to project how the God who was with them would act in the future and had acted in the past. As Friends might say, their sense of God's actions was "experiential." Sure, the Israelites did not know God's grief—nor could they. But they knew their own, both those who were refugees in Babylon and those left to live on the ravaged land, and that was experience enough.

Even the grief of the exiles, though, was not without hope. They looked for someone—a new David perhaps—who would survive the chaos, deliver them, and give them a new beginning. Their traditions told them how to identify this person. It would be someone who had found favor with God, who was righteous, and who walked with God. In writing their version of the flood narrative, they named their model person Noah (from a word that means "comfort") and they made sure he had all three qualifications (see 6:8-9). Yet, in another amazing seesaw of self-disclosure, they had noted earlier that Noah's father was the brutish braggart Lamech (see 4:23-24).

A God of Surprises

My grandson's bedroom notwithstanding, Noah comes late to the scene. Though he will eventually become the fulcrum upon which the whole story pivots, the power of the story is with what precedes him. More than anything else, the flood is a story about God. Already I had been surprised by the God in this story—a God who could regret, and who could be deeply hurt. Another surprise was in store. I would not have seen it, had not Walter Brueggemann pointed it out in his excellent commentary on Genesis.

At issue is the resistant character of humanity. The very first words in the flood story are: "The Lord saw that the wickedness of humankind was great in the earth, and that every inclination of the thoughts of their hearts is only evil continually" (6:5). Later, after the waters have subsided and everyone is safely out of the ark, God makes a kind of internal resolution ("the Lord said in his heart"): "I will never again curse the ground because of humankind, for the inclination of the human heart is evil from youth; nor will I ever again destroy every living creature as I have done" (8:21). God is here acknowledging that, despite the flood, the human heart—the place of knowing and judging—has not changed. And because the human heart has not changed, its impact on the divine heart remains: God is still sorry and grieved. But despite that grief, *God changes*.

For me this was an amazing discovery. The same condition of the human heart that brought on the flood remains after the flood. With the human heart thus unchanged, one could foresee an endless series of floods brought on by repeated grief in the divine heart. But this is a God of the unexpected; if human hearts will not change, then the divine heart will change. The determination is reflected even in the very structure of the text: before and after acknowledging that people remain recalcitrant, God declares: "I will never again" and "nor will I ever again" Human inflexibility is surrounded by divine flexibility.

With that proclamation, God at once expresses—and limits—the divine freedom. An unchanging God would be caught in a cycle of responding to the unchanged human condition; this God has the freedom to change. A totally free God would be without limits; this God accepts a limit: "never again" (8:21). Surely this is no by-the-book God. As Brueggemann notes,

> Israel's God is fully a person who hurts and celebrates, responds and acts in remarkable freedom. God is not captive to old results. God is as fresh and new in relation to creation as he calls us to be with him. He can change his mind, so that he can

abandon what he has made; and he can rescue that which he has condemned.[2]

"Didn't it Rain...?"

It may seem strange that I have hardly mentioned the flood itself. But that's the part of the story everyone already knows, even my five-year-old grandson. Or is it? To understand the flood, we need first to recall the three basic components of creation as mentioned in the first creation story: Sky, Seas, Earth (1:8-10). Add to those components two others that were common in the science of the day: sky windows and underground gates. Each of the five served a practical purpose, especially in a land where water was at a premium. Though the dome of the sky kept the primeval waters above from crashing down and the dry land held the threatening seas at bay, the earth still needed water. It came in the form of rain, which the ancients explained as windows in the sky occasionally opening to let some of the "waters above" fall down. It came also from rivers and lakes, which were thought to exist because flood gates under the earth allowed some of the "waters below" to emerge through openings in the ground.

Come the flood, "all the fountains of the great deep burst forth, and the windows of the heavens were opened" (7:11). With the flood gates and windows thrown open, creation was on the verge not just of inundation but of returning to that formless mass of water, the primordial

---

[2] Brueggemann, Walter *Genesis*, 78.

"deep" from which it was originally called forth (1:2). This does not happen of course, thanks to Noah.

The Crucial Moment

Once the rising waters covered the mountain tops, the ark—with its precious starter kit of "every living thing" (6:19)—was at risk of being crushed against the dome of the sky. It isn't crushed because God intervenes, but *why* does God intervene? The answer is a deceptively simple statement, so simple that it's easily missed: "But God remembered Noah" (8:1). It's hard to overstate the biblical importance of the Hebrew verb that is translated "remembered." The word is *zkr*, and its meanings include: think (about), meditate (upon), pay attention (to); remember, recollect; mention, declare, recite, proclaim, invoke, commemorate. The word appears 288 times in the Bible, with it's meaning reinforced by the frequent use of its opposite—the similarly freighted "to forget" (*skh*), which appears 122 times. This tension between remembering and forgetting, by the people as well as by God, is a major dynamic throughout the Bible.

For God, this remembering is not a sudden "Oh no, I forgot Noah!" Rather it is a shifting of the divine attention from the cataclysmic spectacle of the waters crashing down and roiling up, to the threat this posed to the person with whom God had established a relationship (6:18, 22). Once God remembers (thinks about, meditates on, pays attention to, recollects) Noah, the balance shifts, the waters start to recede, and the world begins to re-emerge.

Without the assistance of the scholarly biblical community, I doubt I would have caught the significance of those deceptively simple four words. Amid all the fanfare of the flood, they are easily overlooked. But they did not escape the inquiring eye of biblical scholars, who see in that straightforward "And God remembered Noah" the key to the whole flood narrative. Everything that comes before leads up to it; everything that follows flows from it. As Brueggemann notes, "It is *remembering* which changes the situation of the world from *hostility* to *commitment*" (page 86, original italics). The closest our translations come to signaling this pivotal text is to make it the start of a new chapter—but current chapter divisions were not added to the Bible until centuries later.

In its detailed exploration of *zkr*, a key sourcebook explains that "in the theological realm *zkr* describes the reciprocal relationship between Yahweh and Israel or individual Israelites" (*The Theological Lexicon of the Old Testament*, 385).The flood story hinges on that relational bond between the Creator and a human creature. At a time when God's heart is grieving over what creation has become, when God regrets having made this world because it has strayed so far from the divine plan, when the Creator determines to "blot out" all that once seemed so promising, the only source of comfort for this sad, regretful, alienated God is Noah. Everything else has cut itself off from any relationship with this God, whose very being is relationship. Just one person emerges in whom the relationship prevails. "Noah found favor in the sight of the Lord" (6:8). No wonder God is so assiduous in preserving this person's life; Noah is the sole survivor of creation as God had intended it. Thus this "righteous man, blameless in his generation; [who] walked with God" (6:9) slips into the story's spotlight.

The flood story begins with God speaking to God's self (6:7), then speaking to Noah (6:13-7:5). After that, God goes silent until the waters have subsided enough that God can tell Noah, "Go out of the ark" (8:16). But the God who stood silently by throughout the crescendo and diminuendo of the flood, speaks again after Noah's sacrifice. As before, the divine words are addressed first to God's self (8:21-22), then to Noah (9:1-17). Both discourses are rich with meaning, but it took the scholarship of biblical experts if for me to uncover that meaning and to mine its depth when all I could see was the surface text.

But is it Quakerly?

Perhaps this sounds un-Quakerly, to rely so heavily on what some Friends might consider "notions"—and notions from outside the Quaker world. Should it not suffice to sit with my Bible and let the Spirit interpret for me? As I indicated earlier, that is precisely what I'm doing: for me, scholars are one source of the Spirit's speaking. Not the ivory tower elites for whom the text is just a puzzle to be solved, but those grounded women and men who take the text also into the marketplace and the ghetto, the halls of government, and the hovels of the oppressed.

I think that Friends who consider mental acumen and academic exchange as antithetical to the Spirit risk being stuck in the mire of individualism and isolated from communal sharing. There was a time, to be sure, when these "notions" were used as bludgeons and prods, rendering almost impossible any Spirit-led interpretation.

For Friends who strive to be open to Truth whatever its source, and who use the clearness of a discerning community as a corrective to individualism—those days are (or should be) over. We need to start listening to the voices that speak from outside our ranks.

Of course we also need to listen to the voices from within—including from within our own faith tradition. Though early Friends railed against the abuse of the biblical text, they also recognized its power. More than that, they were so familiar with it that it was embedded in their speech, even to the point where it now generally goes unrecognized and must be teased out. We should not lightly turn from such a heritage.

Marvels and Mysteries

The post-flood narrative (8:20-9:17) is filled with marvelous and mysterious elements. Foremost, I think, is the change in God's heart to accommodate the unchanged human heart. The text also includes a divine speech (9:1-7) that scholars now see as a new creation story, beginning and ending with the characteristic "be fruitful and multiply" (9:1, 7; see 1:22, 28). In addition, the text includes the Bible's first covenant. This covenant binds God to all humans and all living creatures. Indeed it is a covenant between God and "the earth" (9:14). I find particular significance in the inclusiveness of that covenant; it contextualizes forever any claim of religious exclusivity. The content of the covenant is brief and simple: "Never again." The flood, with all its death and destruction, is no longer a divine option.

Of all the post-flood details, Friends may find particular significance in the sign God chooses to seal the covenant.

"I have set my bow in the clouds, and it shall be a sign of the covenant between me and the earth. When I bring clouds over the earth and the bow is seen in the clouds, I will remember my covenant that is between me and you and every living creature of all flesh; and the waters shall never again become a flood to destroy all flesh. When the bow is in the clouds, I will see it and remember the everlasting covenant between God and every living creature of all flesh that is on the earth." God said to Noah, "This is the sign of the covenant that I have established between me and all flesh that is on the earth." (9:13-17)

Why was a bow chosen as the sign of God's covenant? I could find nothing in my resources that addresses this issue. An online search of the archives of the major biblical journals turned up only a brief 1993 article that argued for translating the word as "rainbow" rather than "bow," but I found no evidence that the scholarly community accepted the argument. True, God's bow is eventually called a "rainbow" and some translations use "rainbow" even in the flood story. But the textual evidence, as I'll indicate, is that the Hebrew word is more accurately translated "bow." Still, why *that* Hebrew word?

Initially, it appears singularly inappropriate. A bow is a weapon, plain and simple. Along with the sling, it is one of the first weapons that allow for killing from a distance that's beyond human strength to reach. As such, the bow is the forerunner of every projectile weapon, be they guns or cannons or bunker-busters. Yet there it is in the text.

The Hebrew word for bow (*qeshet*) occurs 77 times in the Old Testament, and nearly every time in a context of combat. Once, in Genesis 27:3, the context is hunting; once, in Ezekiel 1:28, the context is clouds. Otherwise, the bow is a tool of war—and war in the ancient Near East was as vicious in its day as anything we see now. The Book of Lamentations provides detailed and devastating snippets of what war at that time did to a city and its people: "suffering and hard servitude," "children [taken as] captives," "people... trade their treasures for food," "priests and elders perished," "women eat their offspring," "panic and pitfall... devastation and destruction," "their visage... blacker than soot; skin... shriveled on their bones," "fugitives and wanderers," "our homes [turned over] to aliens," "a yoke on our necks," "women are raped," "the joy of our hearts has ceased; our dancing has been turned to mourning" (Lamentations 1:3, 5, 11, 19; 2:20; 3:47; 4:8, 15; 5:2, 5, 11, 15).

By recognizing what war meant to the Israelites we can begin to appreciate the powerful symbol that the bow must have been for them. How terrifying, then, would be God's own bow: it reaches from horizon to horizon, its string runs the diameter of the earth. Even the Babylonians could not withstand such a weapon. Indeed, it towers over the nations of the world.

But its purpose is not to threaten violence; it is no divine Goliath. It stands instead as a reminder, both to creation and to Creator, of God's covenantal promise never again to destroy the earth with a flood. This most powerful God, who came within inches of letting creation be reabsorbed into the great deep, now forswears such violent action and promises never again to exercise this divine power. What an awesome lesson for those who put their trust in the machinery of violence and war, who, given the chance, would take down God's bow and think themselves righteous for using it.

The Flood Revisited

Perhaps the final biblical word on the flood story belongs to the nameless prophet whose words we read in the latter chapters of the book of Isaiah. The text was likely written in Babylon at the time when the exiles faced the daunting task of rebuilding their city that lay in rubble, and their social fabric that war and deportation had unraveled. The prophet recalls the flood tradition. His imaginative interpretation ties past and present: the past takes on an expanded meaning that the old story never envisioned; the present is recast into a context that links it to an age-old source of confidence. The text is Isaiah 54:7-10, and it warrants close scrutiny.

Before even mentioning the flood, the prophet reapplies to the exiles God's double action of unleashing the flood, then dispelling it. But here he reverses the cause. Instead of human arrogance it is momentary divine distraction

> *For a brief moment I abandoned you,*
> *but with great compassion I will gather you.*
> *In overflowing wrath for a moment*
> *I hid my face from you,*
> *but with everlasting love*
> *I will have compassion on you,*
> *says the Lord, your Redeemer.*   *(Isaiah 54:7-8)*

Next comes the direct reference to the flood, but as an enduring event rather than an ancient story. The words "to me" in the first sentence take this out of the realm of example and into the realm of divine memory.

> *This is like the days of Noah to me:*
>   *Just as I swore that the waters of Noah*
>   *would never again go over the earth,*
> *so I have sworn that I will not be angry with you*
>   *and will not rebuke you.*
>   *(54:9)*

Finally, recalling the time when the waters covered the mountain tops, God pledges a "steadfast love" that survives even such a cataclysmic event. By bringing together the ancient covenant and the resting weapon, God makes a new connection between the two. They now constitute a "covenant of peace," rooted in divine compassion. For me, this is one of most heartfelt and reassuring texts in all the Bible.

> *For the mountains may depart*
>   *and the hills be removed,*
> *but my steadfast love shall not depart from you,*
>   *and my covenant of peace shall not be removed,*
>   *says the Lord, who has compassion on you.*
>   *(54:10)*

Further reading:

Anderson, Bernhard W. *From Creation to New Creation: Old Testament Perspectives.* Minneapolis: Fortress, 1994.

Brueggemann, Walter. *Genesis.* Atlanta: John Knox Press, 1982.

Brueggemann, Walter. *An Introduction to the Old Testament: The Canon and Christian Imagination.* Louisville, Kentucky: Westminster John Knox Press, 2003.

Löning, Karl and Erich Zenger. *To Begin with, God Created: Biblical Theologies of Creation.* Collegeville, Minnesota: Liturgical Press, 2000.

Roop, Eugene. *Genesis,* Scottdale, Pennsylvania: Herald Press, 1987.

Lonnie Valentine is Professor of Peace and Justice Studies at the Earlham School of Religion where he has taught for 16 years. He completed his M.A. in Religion at Earlham and earned a Ph.D. from Emory University. He has two children, Cady and Ben, in their first year at Earlham College. Lonnie has been a peace activist for many years, beginning as a conscientious objector during the Vietnam War.

WAR AND WAR RESISTANCE IN THE OLD TESTAMENT

Lonnie Valentine

In college, I wrote a paper on the Bible entitled "Love the Lord Your God... Or Else." The title summed up how I saw the Bible at that time in my life, and the paper only addressed some New Testament texts. As for the Old Testament, well, it seemed as though even if you loved God you would get whacked in one way or another. However, I also was introduced to process philosophy in college and, through the thought of Alfred North Whitehead, I began to find ways of thinking about my spiritual path, including the Bible, in new ways. One of Whitehead's aphorisms is that humans go through three stages in their relationship to God, "God the void, God the enemy, and God the fellow-sufferer who understands." This development has proved to be true in my engagement with God and the Bible, even including the Old Testament. However, I must admit that God still seems an enemy sometimes!

In this paper, I will present three interrelated approaches to the Old Testament that I hope might be of use to other Quaker pacifists. The first approach is to focus on Jesus as presented in the Gospel accounts as the key that opens the meaning of the rest of the Bible. The second is to recognize that there are multiple voices presented in the Old Testament, including some that support nonviolence. The third is to sever any assumed connection between God and how God is presented in the Bible and rather see the text as a record of human struggles with God. I will take up each of these in turn.

Jesus as Key

Early Friends focused on how Christ was "teaching his people himself" rather than on any biblical text or doctrine. Fox and other early Friends read the Bible frequently, but saw Jesus Christ as the primary source and the Bible as secondary. This did not mean, as with many Friends today, that one could then simply discard the Bible. The Bible was seen as an inspired record of the human witness to Jesus as the Christ. Friends had a method of interpretation that connected the peacemaking Jesus in the Gospels to their own experiences of Christ. Since the Gospel accounts themselves are rooted in the Hebrew Scriptures, this too became a source for Friends. In a similar way, the Bible can be vital in connecting us to those others who have borne witness to God. Just as it is today, there were those who did not see Christ as teaching nonviolence and who made appeals to the Old Testament as justification for wars. Given the importance but not primacy of the biblical text, Friends could and did engage in debates about nonviolence. Their experience was that Christ was leading them to refuse to fight in wars and, instead, to pursue other means to peace. They drew upon the Bible in presenting their case.

Early Friends make this connection between experience, Christ, and the Bible clear in the 1660 declaration "against all fighters in the world." First, they present an analysis of the cause of violence and war: it is human selfishness. Though such selfishness is known experientially, they appeal to the Bible, specifically the first verse of James 4, which connects their experience to James' diagnosis: "Those conflicts and disputes among you, where do they come from? Do they not come from your cravings that are at war within you?"[1] This interconnection of our human experience and the Bible continues as these Friends address how they have experienced Christ and how they relate such experience to the Bible. Probably the best-known portion of the 1660 *Declaration from the Harmless & Innocent People of God Called Quakers* (frequently cited as the first formal statement of the Quaker Peace Testimony) stresses the experiential aspect:

> (T)he spirit of Christ, by which we are guided, is not changeable, so as once to command us from a thing as evil and again to move unto it; and we do certainly know, and so testify to the world, that the spirit of Christ, which leads us into all Truth, will never move us to fight and war against any man with outward weapons, neither for the kingdom of Christ, nor for the kingdoms of this world.[2]

Moreover, this claim comes in the midst of several biblical references that argue that the earliest witnesses to

---

[1] Except as noted, scripture citations are from the New Revised Standard Version.
[2] The full text of the 1660 declaration is available online in the Digital Quaker Collection. Enter at: http://esr.earlham.edu/dqc/index.html

Jesus also understood that he opposed fighting with outward weapons:

> As for this we say to you that Christ said to Peter, "Put up thy sword in his place"; though he had said before that he that had no sword might sell his coat and buy one (to the fulfillment of scripture), yet after, when he had bid him put it up, he said, "He that taketh the sword shall perish with the sword."

The experience of being led by Christ to "seek peace and ensue it" while renouncing participation in war was not solely deduced from scripture. Friends saw Jesus teaching this way of life.

But what of the Old Testament? In the 1660 document, Friends addressed the use of the Old Testament to justify war. First, if the witness to Jesus Christ in the Bible is key, the rest of the biblical text can only be understood from that perspective. Given the early Friends' perspective, the talk of war and rumors of war and God supporting war in the Old Testament is somewhat beside the point. However, Friends did not simply dismiss the Old Testament. Rather they saw Christ and Christ's teachings about war also being taught in the Old Testament.

In approaching the Old Testament, these early Friends drew heavily on the prophetic tradition. Indeed, Christ was seen in line with the Prophets. Early Friends used these texts as a way to strengthen their witness by connecting themselves to Christ, and through Christ, to the prophets who preceded him. In the 1660 declaration, Friends appealed to Isaiah, Zechariah, and Micah. From Zechariah they quote "Not by might, nor by power of outward sword, but by my spirit, said the Lord" (Zechariah 4:6). As one might expect, the vision of Isaiah is primary. The 1660 declaration states:

> (W)e... wait, that by the Word of God's power and its effectual operation in the hearts of men, the kingdoms of this world may become the kingdoms of the Lord, and of his Christ, that he may rule and reign in men by his spirit and truth, that thereby all people, out of all different judgments and professions may be brought into love and unity with God, and one with another, and that they may all come to witness the prophet's words who said, "Nation shall not lift up sword against nation, neither shall they learn war any more." (Isaiah 2:4; Micah 4:3)

This connection between Christ and the Old Testament prophets is deep within Friends' thinking about the Bible. As a Quaker proponent of nonviolence, the witness of Christ as presented in the Gospels also leads me back to the Old Testament prophets.

The Old Testament and Nonviolence

Entering the Old Testament through the Prophets leaves a lot of text untouched and problematic. Does the Old Testament consistently uphold a God of war who commands his people to periodically engage in war? Contrary to what many claim, when read carefully, there is much ambiguity about what God is doing and what those trying to follow God are to do. The easy solution is to dismiss the ugly parts and say these tales in the Bible have nothing to do with God or us. However, it can be enlightening, though challenging, to enter into those difficult texts, even those from which we might recoil.

For the moment, let us put aside the view of Christ as the key for understanding all other biblical texts. What might we see in some of these texts if taken, as best we can, on their own terms? I believe there are at least two fascinating elements. First, the texts dispute with one another and within themselves on issues of violence. Second, we can argue on the grounds of the Old Testament itself (without appeal to the New Testament) that a nonviolent life was the best way of life and that God was present with those who lived nonviolently.

The core of the Old Testament presentation of God as warrior and the people as God's warriors is in the books from Joshua through Second Chronicles. However, there are key texts in this core that in themselves question violence, even as they portray lots of violence. Judges 19-21 is a particularly clear example: there is violence along with a critique of that same violence. In fact, these chapters of Judges can be seen as a turning point in the Old Testament record regarding warfare.

This is the story of the Levite and his concubine. It portrays the gang rape of the concubine and her body being hewn in twelve pieces that are then sent out to the tribes of Israel as a call to come together to wreak vengeance upon those who raped her. Not only do we have human warfare, we have it begun with a horrific assault against an unnamed woman. In much of the tradition, this kind of story (and there are lots more) is read as a general account of the history of Israel: such violence is simply what God and his people need to do sometimes. Such a reading lays the groundwork for excusing violence, including violence against women, and this kind of reading has played havoc in our culture's collective memory. Such readings have contributed to the terror of "Manifest Destiny" in the United States and aligned my country with Israeli violence in holding onto the "promised land" with brutal force. (This is not to deny that there is much in Islam, including the Qur'an's absorption of biblical stories, which also contributes terror in the name of Allah.) If we can understand other ways of reading these texts we can at least offer a dissenting voice to the prevailing assumption that God and warfare—and our wars—all go happily together.

Reading the text as I would another piece of literature, I find that there are elements in the story that lament and resist the run to brutality and war. The story begins with a clue that something might be ready to go wrong; it opens with "In those days, when there was no king in Israel" (Judges 19:1). Having come to this line through the rest of Judges, this is a sign that bad things are going to unfold, and they will so unfold because there is a problem that has not been resolved. Further, something is amiss between the Levite and his concubine; she has fled from him back to her father's house. In some texts it reads she had "played the whore against him" (19:2, KJV), though in most it says that she "became angry with him." The actions of this woman may put us on alert for what is to come. She sees something wrong, just as the narrator at the very beginning tells us that something is amiss.

This sets the stage for the events at her father's house. Her father also sees that something is wrong, and he is worried about what this Levite might do. For several days, there is a tug of war in which the Levite prepares to leave, but is persuaded by his father-in-law to stay another night. Finally, the Levite leaves, and leaves at night. Suggested in the text, and clear in other contexts, is the danger of traveling at night. Another foreboding.

Next, we come to the scene at Gibeah, an Israelite town of the tribe of Benjamin near Jebus (Jerusalem), a town inhabited by "foreigners." The servant asks the Levite to spend the night in Jebus, but, as with his father-in-law, he declines and seeks his own kind in Gibeah, which will take them longer to reach. By the time they reach Gibeah, it is very late and they sit down in the square of the city. Here, an old man offers to take them in, insisting that they not spend the night in the square. Another foreboding, and now the horror begins.

As they are eating and drinking, "men of the city, a perverse lot" demand that the Levite be brought out to them so they "might have intercourse with him" (19:22). The host protests this behavior, since the Levite is a guest, instead offering his own virgin daughter and the man's concubine for their pleasure in exchange for not touching the Levite. There is no narrator's voice here to make a comment, but we can infer that the narrator shares our experience of horror at this behavior. The action of the old man, an Israelite, can fairly be understood as condemned for these actions. Furthermore, the Levite joins in this horrible behavior, pushing his concubine out the door to the waiting men of the city. It is fair to assume that he was fearful and cowardly. In a short while, his own words will confirm this assumption. Do we really think that such behavior would be looked upon with favor? Do we think that ancient readers of this text would fail to see the old man and the Levite as cowards? It is fair to suggest that the narrator believes no comment is necessary on such awful behavior.

The very next scene finds the woman in the doorway of the house as day breaks. In an interesting touch, the narrator adds that her hands were on the threshold of the door. Why would that be added? This entire scene addresses hospitality. The host offers hospitality, the men of the city betray it. Now, the woman's final plea for common hospitality from her own husband and his host is ignored. I do not think it is a minor point that the narrator twice notes that the woman was at the door and adds that her hands are even on the threshold. She has come to the very doorway of the home, indeed is on the doorway, and is again ignored in the midst of her suffering. This is a critique of those who should be her protectors, in essence equating the Levite and his host with the gang of rapists. Further, Judges 19 reiterates the story of Genesis 19 where it is "foreigners" of Sodom and Gomorrah who behave in the same way and who are destroyed by God. Do we think that long-ago readers of this story would not notice this? I think they would.

If the internal critique of all these Israelites' behavior is not clear from the foregoing scenes, it becomes quite clear in the next. Finding his concubine on the threshold in the morning, after resting in peace through the night as she was brutalized, the Levite says to her, "Get up, we are going" (19:28). What a way to address her! Recall in the first part of the story, the Levite wants "to speak tenderly to her and bring her back" (19:3). What kind of tenderness is this? In some texts, it says she is dead when he finds her, but others are ambiguous—it is only reported that she did not answer.

The Levite returns to his home, that symbol of safety. There he takes a knife and cuts her into pieces. We are left to wonder if she was already dead or if the Levite himself killed her. But, does it matter? He is certainly responsible for her death, either by throwing her out to the gang or by finishing her off. As this scene closes Chapter 19, note the Levite's command to the men as he hands out pieces of his concubine: "Thus shall you say to all the Israelites, 'Has such a thing ever happened since the day that the Israelites came up from the land of Egypt until this day?'" (19:30). What is the "thing" to which he refers? Since it is unstated, it is just as legitimate to read the statement as referring to the despicable actions of the Levite as to the behavior of the rapists. After all, we know his behavior and the Israelites do not. The Levite by his actions and his words can be seen as engaging in a cover up and shifting the blame to others.

At the beginning of Chapter 20, the tribes gather and the deceptiveness of the Levite is made clear. The Levite is asked how this all happened, and he replies, "I came to Gibeah that belongs to Benjamin, I and my concubine, to spend the night. The lords of Gibeah rose up against me, and surrounded the house at night. They intended to kill me, and they raped my concubine until she died" (20:4-5). Well, that's one way to describe what happened. However, the preceding text itself shows that the Levite has misrepresented the events, leaving out his own actions. Further, since he doesn't mention throwing his concubine out the door, we can assume he knows his audience would not accept such behavior. Still further, he says she was dead when he found her, but that's not supported by the text.

In the earlier sections of the Book of Judges, judges arose from among the people to deal with external enemies. In this last battle of the book of Judges, we have a civil war. Israelite has turned against Israelite. Further, the terrible irony is that "all the men of Israel" exclaim that the tribe of Benjamin must be punished "for all the disgrace that they have done in Israel" (20:10). From what we have seen, the disgrace falls on all of Israel for following the Levite.

It is important to note that until now there has been no mention of God. People have been following their own ideas about what to do. In fact, that there will be a battle has been decided before anyone thinks to ask God about all this. The question they ask God is telling. Rather than wondering if going to war with one another is such a good idea, they ask God, "Which of us shall go up first to battle against the Benjaminites?" (20:18). That war ought to happen is assumed. The text says that God told them to send Judah. Well, Judah is nearly wiped out. Maybe the first question was the wrong question. With this surprising defeat, they now ask God, "Shall we again draw near to battle?" (20:23). God says yes, and again they are decimated. At this point, the remaining Israelites go back to the Ark of the Covenant and lament. Finally, for the third time, they engage in battle with their own people and prevail. A Pyrrhic victory indeed.

After the war, there is more horror as the now-decimated tribes of Israel try to figure out how to keep the tribe of Benjamin alive. Echoing the scene of the concubine being taken by the men of Benjamin, the other tribes urge the Benjaminites to lay in wait for the women of Shiloh and carry off the young women to be their wives. They do so to get around a self-made rule that no tribe would give their women to marry into the tribe of Benjamin. By allowing them to be taken, the fathers and brothers of the women will not be guilty of permitting intermarriage. In the end, all the men of Israel have behaved badly. To be sure we get the point, the narrator closes this story and the Book of Judges: "In those days there was no king in Israel; all the people did what was right in their own eyes" (21:25).

Immediately following is the peaceful story of Ruth. It is significant that this story follows the book of Judges and was understood to portray an event in the time of the Judges. It has a much different tenor, lifting up the actions of Ruth, a "foreign" woman, as the strong main character who saves her despairing Israelite mother-in-law, Naomi. In contrast to the Levite's concubine, Ruth is a woman with a name who is central to a story of peacemaking. This helps us to remember and critique and move beyond the tragedy of the unnamed woman at the end of Judges. Ruth models another way of addressing fear and threat. Placed as it is, right after Judges, this text offers a telling counterpoint. As in Judges, human actions are the focus, not God's actions, but a very different result happens when humans act justly and with compassion. It is Ruth, a woman and a stranger, who has her name exalted by being named in the lineage of Jesus (Matthew 1:5).

The horror story at the end of Judges only superficially presents war as a way God works in the history of Israel. A careful reading reveals that the rape, murder, and war are condemned within the story itself. What has happened is precisely what Israel ought not to do, and it is not what God wants. The story of Ruth provides this counterpoint in another text. The last verse of Judges seems, however, to point toward the establishment of human kingship and institutionalized warfare under such kings: "In those days there was no king in Israel; all the people did what was right in their own eyes." On the surface, the following books of Samuel and Kings and Chronicles portray the time of Israel's kings and national wars. However, having "no king in Israel" is ambiguous. What might that mean? In 1 Samuel, we see that the issue is this: Who shall be king of Israel, God or a human?

Samuel is born of a barren woman, Hannah, who asks God for a son, and she offers to give this son over for God's service. When she does conceive and give birth, she exults in what God has done and proclaims a message of liberation in Chapter 2: "The Lord makes poor and makes rich; God brings low, and also exalts. God raises up the poor from the dust; God lifts the needy from the ash heap, to make them sit with princes and inherit a seat of honor" (1 Samuel 2:7-8). From Hannah's song to God come Mary's pregnant words in the Magnificat (Luke 1:46-55). With Mary's words, the connection of Jesus to the Old

Testament prophets is now run farther back into the Old
Testament to Hannah and Samuel.

Samuel was no king and understood the desire for a
human king to be a mistake on human terms. More
importantly, in asking for a human king to rule over them,
Israel was forgetting that it should be God who is king. In
a terribly wonderful passage that seems so contemporary,
Samuel warns the people of what kings do:

> *These will be the ways of the king who will reign over you;*
> *he will take your sons and appoint them to his chariots*
> *and to be his horsemen, and to run before his chariots; and*
> *he will appoint for himself commanders of thousands and*
> *commanders of fifties, and some to plow his crop and to*
> *reap his harvest, and to make his implements of war and*
> *the equipment of his chariots. He will take your daughters*
> *to be perfumers and cooks and bakers. He will take the best*
> *of your fields and vineyards and olive orchards and give*
> *them to his courtiers. He will take one-tenth of your grain*
> *and of your vineyards and give it to his officers and his*
> *courtiers. He will take your male and female slaves, and*
> *the best of your cattle and donkeys and put them to his*
> *work. He will take one-tenth of your flocks, and you shall*
> *be his slaves. And in that day you will cry out because of*
> *your king, whom you have chosen for yourselves; but the*
> *Lord will not answer you in that day. (1 Samuel 8:10-18)*

Not exactly a great hymn to warfare and kings. Even
more stunning than this critique of what kings (or
presidents) do, God tells Samuel what the fundamental
issue is: "they have rejected me from being king over
them" (1 Samuel 8:7). The Israelites have rejected God as

their king. From this, the subsequent history of Israel—with kings and the defeats of monarchy and the terrible exiles—follows. Here was a turning point: Samuel says the people turned from their God to being like the other nations, asking for a human king to make them secure against enemies rather than turning to God.

The idea of God as king, in a way far different from human political kings and military leaders, echoes farther back in the biblical narrative to the patriarchs, to Moses and the Exodus. In those distant days, before the tumultuous times of the Judges and the false security of kings, some of the biblical texts portray the people as following God in trust and in nonviolence. Abraham was obedient to God's voice, without promise of physical security. Jacob, the father of the tribes of Israel, seeks peace with his neighbors and decries the violence of his sons, Levi (founder of the tribe of the Levite) and Simeon in Genesis 49:

> *Simeon and Levi are brothers;*
> *weapons of violence are their swords.*
> *May I never come into their council;*
> *may I not be joined to their company—*
> *for in their anger they killed men,*
> *and at their whim they hamstrung oxen.*
> *Cursed be their anger, for it is fierce,*
> *and their wrath, for it is cruel!*
> *I will divide them in Jacob,*
> *and scatter them in Israel.*
> *(Genesis 49:5-7)*

In this speech at the end of his life, Jacob also has bad words for Benjamin, the founder of that other troublemaking tribe in Judges, while he upholds Joseph as exemplifying what a follower of God should do. Joseph, even in the midst of betrayal by his kin, does not seek vengeance and forgives. Jacob says of Joseph that his nonviolent actions were made sure "by the hands of the Mighty One of Jacob, by the name of the Shepard, the Rock of Israel, by the God of your father, who will help you, by the Almighty who will bless you" (Genesis 49:24-25).

The people of Israel began in slavery in Egypt. Joseph was sold into Egyptian slavery by his brothers. God, who protected Joseph, would also protect and liberate the people of Israel. How did that happen? Not by the Hebrew slaves taking up arms in revolt, but by listening to the nonviolent prophet, Moses, that God raised up. Although Moses killed an Egyptian out of anger at what had been done to his people (Exodus 2:11-15), he did not do so again. In the story of the Exodus, God is the warrior who frees the people by acts of nature miracles. The people are simply told to be still and watch. Whatever we are to make of God's actions in all of this, it is critical to see that neither Moses nor the people are urged to take up arms. They are to rely upon a different power and to follow God. When the book of Judges says that Israel had no king, it can be argued that God should have been their king and warrior. Further, God acts through nature, not through human warfare. Humans did not participate in violence for their liberation.

Once we have allowed ourselves to enter into the world of these strange texts, we see many voices being presented and no consistent voice with regard to violence and warfare. Reading these texts as we would any other literature that struggles with ultimate issues, we are confronted with ambiguities and outright contradictions. But rather than being a problem, these are the very aspects of the Bible that can open us up to wrestling with difficult issues.

As we have seen, even as filled with violence and war as the Old Testament is, it also shows that nonviolence is closest to God and God's desires for human beings. Following Jesus back through the prophets that arose as the experiment with monarchy and warfare failed, we can connect to earlier figures like Ruth, Hannah, Samuel, Moses, Joseph, Jacob, and Abraham. These are friends who can help us in our own struggles over how to seek peace in a violent world. These friends can offer us courage and wisdom.

Living Texts, Living Ambiguity

The third step in addressing these strange biblical texts is related to how early Friends engaged the texts. These days, we seem to be caught up in a false dichotomy that claims either the texts must be read literally (whatever that means) or we must reject them altogether. If we get by that, it is hard not to react when the narrator of stories such as those examined here makes claims about what God said or did. We might be able to overlook these claims when God is saying or doing something we like, but this is much more difficult when we are horrified by what we read. In reading other works of literature, we tend to give the narrator's voice the privileged position of telling us what truly is going on or what truly was said. This is contrary to how the stories in scripture debate within and between themselves. There are conflicting voices telling what happened and what God said. It is a great gift to its readers that the biblical text includes these competing voices.

We need not assume that any of the narrators in the Old Testament holds a superior place in their presentation of its characters, including God. Rather, they are like us, trying their best to discern what God is doing and what they ought to do in return. Each of us has made mistakes in understanding what God is doing, so we might allow them some latitude. We might even gain a deeper appreciation of the Bible as we see that it preserved many voices, which conflict with one another about what God is doing and what we should be doing.

Therefore, the final move in how I approach the text is to deny that either the narrators or the words of God are objective truths about what happened, or what God said and did. Rather, the essential question emerges: how am I—how are we—to discern what God is calling us to do now? With this as the question, the burden shifts to us. The Bible becomes something other than the purported words and history of God; it records the struggles of communities of faith over many centuries to understand what God is doing and what we are to do in response. In that way, even those biblical characters and events we do not like can become fellow sufferers with us. More importantly, by engaging the text deeply, we might find we have some friends to join us in the walk towards a more peaceful world.

It might be said that this way of engaging scripture simply allows us to read into the biblical text whatever we want. Of course, that can happen, and it has happened, even when readers think they have a clear sense of what God said and did. However, if we stay with the text as we would other literature that addresses ultimate issues, we might see another relationship emerge. Rather than providing us with an objective account of God's mighty acts in history, we can empathize with all these ancient voices who, like us, wrestled with the question of what God was doing and tried, within the limits of language, to present what they found. The Bible itself recognizes that there are conflicting voices, and presents them for us to engage. Rather than trying to make some definitive theological claims about God, the text invites us into the struggle.

As did people during so much of the Old Testament period, we live in a violent time. We can learn, find support, comfort, and even humor in entering the world of the text. Early Friends saw themselves as joining in that story, as complex and messy as it was. Just as those early Friends did, we can connect the life and teachings of Jesus with his predecessors in the Old Testament: the prophets, Ruth, Hannah, Samuel, Moses, Joseph, Jacob, Abraham, Job, and others. Peacemaking is a hard path, but we have had company for a long, long time.

Annotated Bibliography

For those who want to do more exploration of the Old Testament, let me suggest the following.

In terms of warfare, I highly recommend the 1991 edition of Gerhard von Rad's classic study translated and edited by Marva J. Dawn and John H. Yoder, with a useful historical introduction by Ben. C. Ollenburger and a bibliography by Judith E. Sanderson:

von Rad, Gerhard. *Holy War in Ancient Israel.* Grand Rapids, Michigan: William B. Eerdmans Publishing, 1991.

I can suggest two books on war in the Old Testament. The first is a traditional, fairly technical, historical critical approach to war in the Old Testament by a Mennonite; the second provides a more recent treatment of the topic:

Lind, Millard C. *Yahweh is a Warrior: The Theology of Warfare in Ancient Israel.* Scottdale, PA: Hearld Press, 1980.

Niditch, Susan. *War in the Hebrew Bible: A Study in the Ethics of Violence,* New York & Oxford: Oxford University Press, 1995.

Three excellent books that give positive readings of the text in relation to issues of violence are:

Birch, Bruce. *What Does the Lord Require? The Old Testament Call to Social Witness.* Philadelphia: Westminster Press, 1985.

Brueggemann, Walter. *Living Toward a Vision: Biblical Reflections on Shalom.* Philadelphia: United Church Press, 1982.

Brueggemann, Walter. *The Prophetic Imagination,* Minneapolis: Augsburg Fortress Press, 1978.

In terms of literary approaches to the Bible, look at two by Phyllis Trible. The first is considered a classic, while the shorter and less technical second book provides an easier way in:

Trible, Phyllis. *God and the Rhetoric of Sexuality*, Philadelphia: Fortress Press, 1978.

Trible, Phyllis. *Texts of Terror: Literary-Feminist Readings of Biblical Narratives*, Philadelphia: Fortress Press, 1984.

Esther Mombo works at St. Paul's Theological College in Limuru, Kenya, an ecumenical institution that teaches theology and other courses to a number of denominations including Quakers. She teaches History and Women's Studies and serves as the Academic Dean of the college. In addition, she is on the board of Friends Theological College, a Quaker institution in Kaimosi, Kenya.

Esther's research focuses on issues of women and the church. Her Ph.D. thesis looked at the role of women in what was then known as East Africa Yearly Meeting of Friends (the Quaker Church in Kenya). She is a member of the Circle of Concerned African Women Theologians.

Esther is a member of Getembe Monthly Meeting, Bware Yearly Meeting. She has facilitated and spoken at a number of Quaker gatherings in Kenya, especially at Yearly Meetings.

RAPE: THE INVISIBLE CRIME

Esther Mombo

The Story of Phoebe

When I was a teenager, my aunt Phoebe was raped. She had a mental breakdown when she was in her mid-thirties, and it is only now that I am able to connect the two.

Phoebe was about seventeen years old and in primary school. One Saturday my grandmother sent her to go and visit her elder sister in another village and to take some foodstuffs with her because she had people working in her garden. Phoebe went, and we did not see her until the next day after coming out of hospital. On her way to the sister's house Phoebe was met by a man who was said to be mentally disturbed; he caught her and took her to a bush and raped her repeatedly. He left her there helpless. Some passersby rescued Phoebe and helped her to her sister's house.

Word came home of what had happened to Phoebe, and my grandmother rushed to see her. Together with others they managed to take Phoebe to a local clinic where she was treated for the physical injury she had suffered. Then she returned home. The man who raped her was later found and arrested but nothing was done to him; he was released after his family requested that the matter be settled out of court. My grandfather tried to follow the case, but he was told that it was shameful to talk about such things in public. His daughter was an adult and could be married, and he should be grateful that she is alive. Thinking about it now it was not easy to deal with such cases then especially if there was no one to follow the matter up keenly.

For a few days that followed, Phoebe quietly sat outside the house on a mat, occasionally chasing the flies that surrounded her because of the bad odour from her physical injury. She was quiet, and no one talked to her much other than ensuring that she was given food and water to bathe. Her sisters, her mother, and other women in the home were all shocked about the event but talked in low tones. What if she was pregnant? What about venereal disease? What will happen to her in the future? My grandfather blamed my grandmother for sending Phoebe, and others blamed Phoebe for taking the route she took. No one took time to talk to Phoebe and hear what she was going through. She was left alone to recover, and she did recover from her physical injuries, but not from her emotional damage. She has continued to be a wounded woman.

Talk about Phoebe was in low tones, with the sigh of relief that she was alive. Those who wished to know what she was suffering from were given the name of some disease rather than told of the rape for fear of her reputation as a girl in the village. The life of the home went on as normal, but Phoebe sat on a mat each day with her internal pain. After recovering from her physical injuries, Phoebe went back to school. She finished and, after completion, she was hired as a teacher. Not long after, she was pregnant by another teacher. She was married off fast because if she were not she would lose her job. Was she raped again to become pregnant? Did she choose to marry this man or did she do it to cover her shame and to retain her job?

It was a relief to the family when she got married and lived what was viewed as a normal life. Later, she had a mental breakdown, which also was a shock to the family and was also treated with suspicion. It was hidden from being known because, again, mental illness is not made public in this culture. Here was Phoebe, again suffering, and the suffering was being hidden. She was given treatment, both herbal and modern, but only the husband knew what he was treating. Looking back, Phoebe never became active in church activities even though she attended church. Today Phoebe has grown-up children; she is not stable emotionally; and she reacts badly to situations of suffering or events that shock. While the family is aware that she has some emotional problems, no one has ever bothered to find out the root cause of all these. She is at times kept away from places of conflict or trauma.

Being a Quaker home, and my grandmother being a preacher, we read the Bible every night and prayed. There was no connection between what had happened to Phoebe and the Bible we read or the prayers we said asking God to heal her. It was only when I began reading the Bible myself that I realised what my aunt had gone through and why our family treated her the way we did.

Looking back, several questions have remained unanswered: Why was the subject of rape not discussed? Why was there a split between what had happened to Phoebe and the life of the home including prayers and

Bible study? Why was Phoebe isolated? Reading the Bible, especially the stories about rape, has helped me to talk about the story of Phoebe. It took so long for me to discover these portions of scripture, and I have wondered why they were included in the Bible.

I came to realise that the stories of the women in the Bible are not different from those of women in my time and country. According to a national survey on the public and private abuse of women in Kenya, it is estimated that every thirty minutes a woman is raped and that one in every six women between fifteen and seventy years has experienced physical or sexual violence.

In a context that is heavily influenced by Christianity and its scriptures, how do I read the Bible and especially the portions on rape that I have chosen to write about? I was brought up with the view that the Bible was the authoritative and normative witness to divine revelation among the Christians, and especially for the Quaker Christians among whom I was born and lived my life. The Bible provides Christianity with its dominant narratives, images, and symbols. These are taken up in preaching, teaching, prayer, and doctrine and thus play a part in shaping the religious consciousness of believers.

Quakers in Kenya

Quakers in Kenya come from a very strong biblically-based background. The Friends Church in Kenya was founded by American Quaker missionaries who had been influenced by the Great Revival, which began to affect the Quakers from 1860 onwards. The Friends Africa Industrial Mission, which sent the first missionaries to Africa in 1902, aimed at founding a church where people were converted to the Christian faith. Like other Quakers, those in Kenya did not subscribe to a confessional doctrinal statement. The theological presuppositions were based on the revival principles, which had brought an intense concern for the salvation of souls. After conversion it was important that the people had the Bible translated into their language so that they could read it for themselves. The Bible became central to the work of evangelism and literacy, which went hand in hand. Writing about the work of mission at the time Arthur Chilson noted that, "The mission stations had thousands of scholars and the Bible was the basic textbook. In every session," he said, "there was a Gospel service in which the Bible truth was presented and the sinners urged to seek forgiveness of sins. Education was used as a means of conversion of the individuals."

It is against this background that I was born and brought up. My grandmother, who was among the first women converts to Quaker Christianity, could read the Bible fluently. She taught her grandchildren the centrality of the Bible in the Quaker faith. She had learnt the Bible by heart, and she narrated to us, her grandchildren, the stories of creation, the exodus, the exile, the gospel narratives of Jesus, and his significance in the Christian faith. Each of the stories she told was in relation to the greatness of God and what it meant to believe. I, therefore, grew up understanding that the Bible was central to the way Quaker Christians did things.

Reading the Bible as an African Woman

As a theological student, I began to read the Bible for myself and to interpret it. I was introduced to various methods of interpreting the Bible beginning with the text-centred approach (or textual hermeneutic) of the early church, the author-centred approach (or historical critical method) of European history, and the reader-centred approaches pertaining to the currently popular variables of gender, race and economic class. This third approach is the one that has influenced me in the reading of the Bible, and it is the way I use to look at the texts that I deal with below.

So what is the reader-centred approach? In this approach, the Bible is seen not merely as an ancient text offering intellectual recreation in terms of constructing an ancient history, but as scripture to which contemporary men and women can turn to solve their real-life problems. This methodology has put the Bible into a sharper focus than it was before. The focus has now shifted from the objective to the subjective, from the descriptive to the normative, from problem analysis to problem solving, from theoretical to applied. This methodology has influenced me because, rather than being involved in the recovery of the author's original meaning or the context of the biblical authors, the reader-centred methodology insists on finding similarities between the Bible and the context of the reader. This methodology has been embraced by liberation theologians in their quest for reading and understanding the Bible in a manner that can liberate women and men from oppression on the basis of gender, race, and class. It is also a methodology that most African women theologians have embraced in order to critically analyse the way the Bible has been used in the treatment of women.

In reading the Bible, it is clear that it was written and created by men in patriarchal cultures and largely reflects a patriarchal world order. Women reading the Bible find issues such as the invisibility and the inferiority of women in it. There is also the sexism of the process of translation and interpretation. It is in this context that some readers have wondered whether the Bible can ever liberate women from a patriarchal, male-chauvinistic system of oppression. Others challenge the traditional understanding of the Bible as the revealed word of God if it appears to legitimise and even commands female suppression. If one uses text-centred or author-centred approaches to the study of the Bible, the challenges raised are real and true. However those who embrace a reader-centred approach, like most African women theologians, would argue differently. Grace Imathiu for example observes that

> African biblical hermeneutics interested in the experience and hopes of African women must take seriously a reading strategy that takes into account the text's silent characters—a reading strategy that reads between the lines, using women's experience as a resource.[1]

---

[1] Imathiu, Grace, "Reading Between the Lines: Power, Representation and Luke's Acts" in Nyambura J. Njoroge and Musa W. Dube (Eds.) *Talitha Cum! Theologies of African*

Justin Ukpong also emphasizes that the main focus of interpretation must be on the communities that receive the text rather than on those that produced the text. The specific culture or life experience each community brings to the Bible is, on this view, our main resource for interpreting it effectively.[2]

Knowing the weight of the Bible on African Christianities, Quakers included, African women have embraced the Bible and use it to analyse their particular situation of triple sexism: sexism in the African culture, sexism in the colonial culture, and sexism in the biblical culture. Mercy Amba Oduyoye argues that, as a woman, she feels the weight of sexism but she is empowered when she reads the stories of the Exodus, the Exile and other biblical motifs where "the least" are recognised and affirmed or are empowered to critique the social injustice. Despite the entrenched patriarchal and ethnocentric prepositions of the Bible, it is still a book that she cannot dispense with so long as she remains in the Christian community.[3] Along the same lines Musimbi Kanyoro observes that

---

Women, Pietermaritzburg, South Africa: Cluster Publications, 2001, 27-39

[2] Ukpong, Justin, "Developments in Biblical Interpretation in Africa: Historical and Hermeneutical Directions" in Gerald West (Ed.), *The Bible in Africa*. Leiden: Brill, 2000, 11-28.

[3] Oduyoye, A. M. (ed.), *Transforming Power: Women in the Household of God*, Proceedings of the Pan-Africa Conference

The Bible is a message of liberation for African woman, much as it is also used to deny their freedom. For women to find justice and peace through the texts of the Bible, they have to try and recover the women participants as well as their possible participation in the life of the text. Secondly, women will need to read the scriptures side by side with the study of cultures and learn to recognise the boundaries between the two. Such recognition will help women to interpret biblical passages within the proper hermeneutical understanding of us and our contexts as Christian women being apologetic to the culture set-up in which the message of the biblical passage has found its audience.[4]

The thrust of the above quotes seems to be that the Bible as such is not an instrument of oppression of women, but rather a lopsided interpretation of the Bible, which has been vested with ulterior motives. It is true to say that in any hermeneutic of the Bible we have to determine what is the fundamental truth and what are the cultural expressions through which this truth has been expressed. There is truth, the word of God in the Bible, but it comes dressed in the trappings of a particular culture, a particular world-view. In re-reading the Bible, we have to make efforts to discern between the divine and the human elements in it. In reading the Bible, there is a fundamental

---

of The Circle of Concerned African Women Theologians, Accra-North, Ghana: Sam-Woode Ltd., 1997, 4-6.

[4] *Ibid*

truth on the equality of human beings as stated in Genesis
1:26-27 and Galatians 3:28. This, the Quakers have also
taught, hence their reputation of being a religious society
which lays emphasis on the "priesthood of all believers"
and thus the equality of men and women. One would then
conclude that reading the difficult texts would help me as
a Quaker to use them to challenge injustice of any sort.

It is against this background that I look at the stories of
Phoebe, Dinah, and Tamar. The story of Phoebe is from my
family today, while those of Dinah and Tamar are from the
Bible, which is my family of old. But from whatever
period, these stories are for women in most parts of our
society today. These stories are about patriarchy, sexism,
double standards, and the silent pain of many who have
been raped.

Genesis 34: The Story of Dinah

In Genesis 34 we read about Jacob's family getting
settled in the Promised Land. Jacob had been re-united
with Esau, and his new name was Israel. Jacob had
actually bought a piece of land in Shechem and built an
altar for the Lord. In the midst of settling down we read
the bitter incidence of violence first through the rape of
Dinah, Jacob's daughter. Dinah was the daughter of Leah,
first and less-loved wife of Jacob. Her brothers include
Simeon and Levi. Dinah went to visit the Canaanite
women, and during the visit, a local prince—son of the
ruler of the town—raped her. The prince fell in love with
her and decided to marry her. He asked his father, Hamor,
to arrange a marriage and the father went and approached
Dinah's father, Jacob, on the same. Jacob waited until his

sons came from the field. The act of rape did not please the family of Dinah.

When Dinah's brothers heard what had happened "they were filled with grief and fury" but they pretended that it was all-well. They accepted that Dinah should marry the prince on condition that all the men in the city get circumcised. The men of the city got circumcised but, while they were still in pain from the operation, Simeon and Levi attacked the town, killed every male in it, and took their sister from Shechem's house. Their father, Jacob, admonished them but they felt justified. They said "Should he have treated our sister like a prostitute?"

As a result of Dinah's rape, there was an outbreak of violence when Simeon and Levi chose to attack and kill the men when they were recuperating from the pain of circumcision. The other brothers co-operated in plundering the town, taking everything that was there, including the women and the children and making them their prey. The sons of Jacob made the others suffer because they did not consider the Canaanites as people.

The story stands on its own in Genesis, with no apparent connection to what precedes it or what follows it. Dinah is not mentioned again in the Bible, except as a name in a long list of the descendants of Jacob, which includes grandchildren as well as children (Genesis 46:15). But perhaps Dinah has no children because she did not get married. In the Old Testament society, a woman who was known not to be a virgin at marriage could not expect to find a husband. (Deuteronomy 22:20-21). If a woman was raped, the rapist was forced to marry her (Deuteronomy 22:28-29). Dinah's rapist was willing to marry her and to pay whatever was required, but her family did not accept it, and there was no one who would marry her.

From reading the story, we realise that Dinah is an independent woman, who chooses to visit her neighbours even if they are not members of her tribe, and she paid a price for it. After her rape she is treated more as an object than a person. Shechem keeps her in his house as he negotiates for her marriage. She appears not to be consulted about anything.

The brothers seem to have been caring towards her: they fought for her, yet there is no mention of concern for her as a person. They do not go to comfort her, but waited until they can make a revenge on the rapist. In Genesis 34:7 we read, "They were filled with grief and fury, because Shechem had done a disgraceful thing in Israel by lying with Jacob's daughter—a thing that should not be done." The anger of these brothers was not so much about the hurt done to Dinah as the disgrace brought to the family honour. This family honour was invested in the chastity of Dinah. This dishonour far outweighed the behaviour of the men in the family. The males were justified in defending their family honour, even by deceit and murder. Their sister's welfare was only incidental: her significance was as a piece of family property, which had been violated.

We realise that after the rape Dinah becomes the object of actions rather than their subject. She does not do much, but things are done to her. We do not know her emotions, nor is her story told. Dinah no longer has the power to make of herself anything; her sexual identity is defined by the choices of men. This is similar to what happens to some victims of rape today. There is a dilemma on what to do because reporting the case to the police has its own consequences. It may result in other physical or emotional assault. Growing up in my village we were advised not to go to a police station if it was late because we would be molested. Even if the police are expected to protect, it is not usually the case. Like Dinah, women who are raped today become objects of other people's investigations if they choose to speak up. Very often their feelings about the whole matter are ignored and devalued, and their identity is shaped by the decisions and actions of other people.

Like Dinah women who are raped today face a life of isolation, not finding support even from the church. In the context of HIV/AIDS, a rape is comparable to being sentenced to death. But the worst is the double standard, which is similar to what we have in society today. The man who rapes a woman may find himself facing a certain disapproval—or he may be proud of and praised for his sexual prowess. A woman, on the other hand, who is involved in any kind of extra-marital sexual activity is stigmatised. Whether she acts on her own free will or is forced into it is often irrelevant. It is true to note that one of the factors that leads to the appalling violence of this story is the double standard taken for granted by the sons of Jacob.

Just as in the Bible, there are many examples today where one violent act is used as an excuse, a pretext, for greater violence. The superficial reason given is revenge: "we have to act to punish them for their violence against us." But in fact the actions taken go far beyond any conceivably appropriate kind of revenge, and those claiming vengeance manage to grab property, possessions, or land that perhaps they wanted for years. This violent overreaction is typical of many abusive situations from the domestic to the international scene. For example "she was dressed indecently so she was raped" or "she served cold dinner so she was beaten." Are these real reasons, or is someone frustrated? Do they have resentment inside them and so they acted in this manner? Internationally, we hear things such as "they have weapons of mass destruction, so we will bomb them to bits." The weapons of mass destruction are not discovered. Was that the issue or was it about other issues? Unfortunately, each act of violence leads to another; it does not stop.

How does one read the story of Dinah in a context where men dominate women and female personhood is submerged in a male-dominated society? Why is this story included in scripture? It is easy for this story to be read and interpreted in a way that blames women who are raped, as though it is their fault. The story helps to raise issues, which can help empower victims of rape.

First, it was not Dinah's fault that she was raped. She was doing what she loved to do—visit and familiarise herself with the local community. She did not choose to be confined in the home like the other women of the patriarchs were. She became a victim of patriarchal violence for not being a member of the local community. Dinah here represents many women in society who are refugees for one reason or another and who are vulnerable to attack.

Other positive things in this story include the disapproval of violence. Shechem's act in raping Dinah is strongly condemned especially in verse 7 quoted above. And there is condemnation of the sons of Jacob, too. The trap they set for Shechem and Hamor is described as deceitful, which is negative in biblical terms. In Psalm 5:6 we read that "the Lord abhors the bloodthirsty and deceitful." The use of the word deceitful indicates that their actions are unacceptable to God. The nature of the deceit is also significant. As a basis of their trick, they used circumcision, the sacred sign of the covenant which God had given to Abraham (Genesis 17:10-11). To the Jews, circumcision is more than a ritual; it is a constant reminder of their basic faith, their covenant with God. To use this as a means of tricking their enemy devalues and debases the sign God had given them.

So this re-telling has two important results. First, it recovers the story of Dinah and gives us insights into the nature and results of rape. In so doing, it exposes the relationship between that act of violence and the violent attack on the city of Shechem and on its women, children, and men. Second, in today's context, where sexual abuse and rape is on the increase, women need to hear and tell the stories of the Bible that condemn it.

2 Samuel 13: The Story of Tamar

Apart from Michal, daughter of Saul (1 Samuel 18:27), and Bathsheba (2 Samuel 11:27), King David had at least six wives (2 Samuel 3:2-5). Amnon, son of Ahinon of Jezreel, is his first son. Tamar and Absolom are sister and brother, the children of David and Maacah. So Amnon is half brother of Tamar, with whom he thinks he has fallen in love. Maybe this affected him physically as well as mentally, and he fell sick. One of his relatives, Jonadab, came to his aid, and together they plotted how to get Tamar alone with Amnon.

Tamar went to Amnon's bedside on the orders of King David, and made him cakes to help him feel better. But Amnon and his crafty friend Jonadab had devised this plot to trap her. After preparing the cakes, Tamar realised what he was up to, and it was not possible for her to escape. She tried to negotiate her way out of rape by presenting four arguments to persuade Amnon to stop. First, it was against the Israelite custom to do such a thing. Second, such an act would disgrace her. Third, his reputation would be ruined, and he would be "a wicked fool." Fourth, she pointed to the fact that if he sought it, King David would give her to him in marriage. But Amnon did not listen to any of this, and in the circumstance nothing could stop him from raping her. Amnon overpowered her and fulfilled his desire.

After the act, Amnon's lust for Tamar turned to loathing. He wanted to chase her away, but she was not like a disposable object. Tamar did not leave easily because she knew that, as was the custom of the time, he should marry her. She put up a defence by saying that sending her away was worse than what he had done. Amnon was not willing to listen to her and insisted that she be put out of his house through the help of his servant. When Tamar came in the house, he wanted the servant out, but now he wanted the servant in and Tamar out.

Having been put out of the house, she did not wish to hide what had happened to her or to remain silent about it. She was ready to make known what had happened to her rather than to pretend that nothing had happened. She left Amnon's house and showed visible signs of what has been done to her: the torn dress, the ashes on her hair, the tears. Hence her brother Absolom realises what has happened.

When her father, King David, heard about the incident, he was angry but he did nothing to help her. In this story, Tamar is never identified as David's daughter, showing how the relationship between the father and the son was stronger than the father and the daughter. Tamar remained a desolate woman at her brother's house. This act of violence led to more violence when Absolom had Amnon killed. But this murder does nothing for Tamar. Nothing can restore her virginity, and its loss has wrecked her life. Like Dinah, she is never mentioned in the Bible again.

The story of Tamar combines incest and domestic violence. Why is such a story included in the Bible? The story shows that any woman is susceptible to violence. It does not matter whether she is poor or rich. The story reveals the brutality done to women and those who are violated. For Tamar, hope for a normal life is shattered. We find in this story how men conspire to violate a woman and how they try to silence her in order to safeguard the name of the family. Tamar, however, is a victim of rape who raises her voice and makes the issue known. In a Kenyan context, where the cases of incest are on the increase due to social change, this story is empowering to those who are violated. Many times, the victims go through a very painful psychological trauma but the family more often does not take the case seriously. Some times, those who reveal violations or sexual abuse are silenced and this increases their pain.

As in the case of Tamar, today's victims are abused in known environments not only by strangers, but by family and friends. Their efforts to resist are met with the same kind of treatment that Tamar received. The victims are not asked about their treatment, but unilateral decisions are taken about them.

In the case of Tamar we see how she is not counted as a person but as an object, the property of men. This does not mean that if women are treated as property the pain they undergo, the terror and agony, should be treated lightly. Neither can one argue that the Bible does not take the incidents seriously. Tamar's actions of raising her voice both before she was abused and also after are clear testimony to this.

Reflection

These three stories have similarities in showing rape can happen to anyone and a rapist can be anyone. Rape takes place in all places, including the palace. Rapists are not necessarily strangers; they are relatives and/or friends. More than this, the stories raise deep issues such as the silence that surrounds rape and how the victims are forced to cope. The victims are treated as objects as their personhood is violated. There is also the abuse of power and authority and the double standards in dealing with rape cases as men, in some instances, are left to go free or are covered.

The stories of rape show how women who are raped are silenced instead of being helped to speak up and to deal with the rape. For example when Tamar tried to raise her voice about what had happened to her, she was silenced to protect the family name. Phoebe did not even have a chance to raise her voice; even those who would have spoken on her behalf did it in low tones. For these women, the terror, shame, and the overwhelming power of the males was unbearable.

These three stories of raped women show a bleak future for the women. If a woman is unmarried when she is raped, it is not easy to get married. Phoebe has lived a life with emotional problems; Dinah and Tamar live miserable lives, as no one is willing to marry them. Phoebe became a mother in a society that forced it on her and she has lived in the shadow of married life. Her mental and emotional stress has been treated lightly, and she is hidden if it causes family disgrace. Dinah and Tamar lost out on being mothers in a society where that was considered the ideal for each woman. They became the social outcasts of that society. For married women who are raped, the situation is not any better. Even if they stay in a marriage, they still live with trauma and agony as society appears not to understand what the rape victim is going through. In the current climate of HIV/AIDS, a rape may indeed be a death sentence.

The stories also reveal the cultural context of both the biblical and Kenyan societies. The cultural context is that of male dominance because men have the power to do what they wish to do. Amnon, David's son, is not punished but protected both by his victim's father and by the customs of the society, which are lenient to men. In

Dinah's case, it is the men who go for each other, and she is left to live with her pain.

What happened to the three women in these stories is a violation of their humanity. They did not do anything to provoke the violence. They lacked support from family and the community at large. If there had been support, they could have shared their harsh experiences. By speaking about Phoebe, Dinah, and Tamar the invisibility of the injustice done to them is made visible.

The Quaker community in Kenya frequently ignores these problems, choosing to remain silent. But no longer can this situation continue, for the women and other victims of violence are becoming courageous and raising their voices. The Quaker Church has to take a stand, affirm its solidarity with those that have been violated, and challenge the forces that perpetuate this kind of violence. The Quaker community needs to become the voice of the voiceless. As emphatic listeners and catalysts for change, the community can enable others to revive their lives, re-establish relationships, be reconciled in community, and face the difficult realities of life.

Conclusions

This paper is about reading the Bible as a Kenyan Quaker, and I began by what has influenced me to read the Bible and the reader-centred approach that I use. Thus, the two Bible stories I chose to read are not just ancient texts but incidents of women who continue to be raped in Kenya today, as my family story shows. Rape, as noted above, occurs in all cultures, in all social classes, against women of all ages. In my context, rape is combined with other forces such as economic degradation and religious silence. It is also linked to political and military influences. The laws, which make the defence of women nearly impossible, protect the rapists.

I am bound to ask, where is God? Why does God not intervene to prevent Shechem from raping Dinah? Why does God not act beforehand to warn Tamar? Why does God not shield Phoebe from a brutal man along the way? Why does God not send angels, to comfort and support these women in the wilderness of their desolation as he did to Hagar? (Genesis 16:7-12; Genesis 21:17-19). This is the experience of many, many suffering women. The silence of God is part of the experience of so many who face desolation.

As a Kenyan Quaker, I read these stories with the view that humanity is a fallen race, one that knows what God expects but does the opposite. The stories are a lesson to all who care to read and act. First, listen to the experiences of the victims from their own point of view and free of any prejudices. This will provide opportunity for the victim to express her inner feelings without any fear of judgment. This, in itself, will be a process of healing for the victims. Second, stand in solidarity with the victims and challenge the powers that provide opportunity to the abuser to abuse and the authority that tends to protect the interests of the abuser.

This, the Bible is telling me.

Howard R. Macy is Professor of Religion and Biblical Studies at George Fox University. Mostly, he teaches in Old Testament studies with special interest in Psalms and the Prophets, but also has keen interest, teaches, and writes about Friends matters, worship, and Christian spirituality. He also taught at Earlham College and Friends University. He served Smith Neck Friends Meeting (NEYM) and Reedwood Friends Church (NWYM) and as yearly meeting staff for Northwest and Indiana Yearly Meetings. A recorded minister in Northwest Yearly Meeting, he is a member of Newberg Friends Church, Newberg, Oregon where he is actively engaged in worship ministries. A regular contributor to *Quaker Life* magazine for twenty-five years as well as to the *Evangelical Friend* and *Quaker Religious Thought*, he has spoken and taught widely in local meetings, conferences and yearly meetings across EFI and FUM. His book *Rhythms of the Inner Life* engages themes of spirituality and the Psalms.

LEARNING TO READ THE PSALMS

Howard R. Macy

To speak of "reading" the Psalms risks distorting from the outset how to approach them. We are prone to read informationally rather than transformationally, to read "objectively," at a distance, merely indulging our curiosity and desire to control. Coming to know the Psalms requires more. It requires deep listening and engagement and these, at their best, in the context of the community of faith.

Rather than seeing the Psalms simply as "texts," we more accurately approach them as the prayers and songs of a worshipping community going back as much as three thousand years. Jews and Christians have used them in temples and synagogues, homes and catacombs, cathedrals and monasteries, prayer groups and private devotion, and they still endure as the unrivalled community resource for prayer and worship. I join with those who believe that the Spirit of God guided in creating, preserving, and recognizing the value of these songs that have become scripture. I also affirm that the Spirit continues to teach through and enliven the Psalms to lead us to encounter with God.

The Psalms do not teach in as direct a way as the Torah, the Prophets, the Gospels, or the Epistles. Rather than words from God, in some sense, they are words to God. They are words of prayer—praising, pleading, trusting, thanking, complaining. Yet, as we understand that it is God alone who teaches us to pray, attending to and entering these songs opens to us the geography and language of prayer. The Psalms give us words we could not find, permission to pray in ways that we scarcely dared, assurance that, even in dark times, God draws near in love and power.

In reflecting on how I approach the Psalms, I find that I use three complementary but distinct approaches. The first is analytical or exegetical, the second is imaginative, and the third is prayerful. Because I tend to impose my own time and culture on the Psalms, I need to explore how their first singers and hearers understood them. Because the Psalms are poetry and song, I need to see and hear them with a receptive imagination. Because the Psalms have their life in the heart of worship, I must learn to enter them in prayer.

Exploring the Psalms

For me, careful exegesis is a valuable approach to engaging the Psalms. Simply put, exegesis uses a variety of analytical tools to discover how the original singers and hearers of these songs might have understood them. Contrary to some contemporary approaches to interpretation, this assumes that we can discover what the first writers intended to say and that when we use these songs we should be guided by their message. Disciplined study can both forestall misleading interpretations and open refreshing insights that we might miss.

The work of analysis belongs to a community of readers, some of whom bring special technical skills. Much of this work is available in accessible Bible commentaries for readers who want to explore it. One such technical skill is text criticism, which tries to establish as accurately as possible the original reading of the biblical text. Good translations and study Bibles clue ordinary readers about where this makes a difference in the text. For example, in Psalm 100:3 modern interpreters believe the reading "It is he that made us, and we are his" is more accurate than the traditional rendering "and not we ourselves."

Analyzing literary forms can also increase understanding. For example, the careful work of form criticism has identified specific forms for praise, thanksgiving, and lament songs and how they are organized internally. I have found helpful spiritual insight in the way that the lament song gathers complaint, confessions of trust, pleas for help, and expressions of praise. The form of the hymn itself also teaches the ways of worship.

We can also explore the Psalms by looking into their historical and cultural backgrounds. Unlike much of the Old Testament, we can rarely know the specific circumstances of most of the Psalms, though no doubt this actually contributes to their continuing timelessness and timeliness. We can reconstruct in some measure, though, the circumstances and activities of worship—architecture, instruments, ritual practices, processions, shouting, dancing, antiphonal singing. With this we can learn to enter into the spirit and majesty of lines like "Lift up your heads, O gates! And be lifted up, O ancient doors! That the

King of glory may come in" (Psalm 24:7).[1] Similarly, when we learn that shepherding language in ancient Israel referred to not only green pastures but also royal courts, it can add depth to "The Lord is my shepherd" (Psalm 23) and similar phrases. So can learning about shepherding itself.

One of my favorite analytical tools is exploring the meanings of words, trying to reach behind the limitations of translation. (Almost anyone can do this by comparing translations and using study tools such as commentaries and theological wordbooks.) It deepened my understanding, for example, when I discovered that the same Hebrew word translated "meditate" in Psalm 1 is translated "plot" in Psalm 2. Suddenly it made a sharp contrast between giving your focused attention to living in God's way (Psalm 1) and steadily focusing your attention to rebelling against God's purposes (Psalm 2). Similarly, I have loved with many others the assurance that God's "goodness and mercy shall follow me all the days of my life" (Psalm 23:6). But it still cheers me to know that the word "follow" has more to do with pursuing than tagging along behind. To be pursued by God's "mercy" (Hebrew *hesed*), God's never-give-up-on-you love, is reassuring, indeed.

Seeing the Psalms

Reading analytically offers fine rewards, and it would be easy to stop there. For me as a person trained in biblical studies the texts often tease me to explore yet one more

---

[1] Bible verses are from the New Revised Standard Version.

word or phrase, usually with profit. Others, less tempted by such habits of study, may be satisfied by the informational reading that they use to manage most of their everyday reading of newspapers, reports, textbooks, junk mail, and more. We tend to scan, skim, and read words well but superficially. That kind of reading probably serves us well, but it won't lead us adequately into the Psalms.

The main drawback of informational reading is that the Psalms are poetry, and you don't read poetry like the classifieds, obituaries, box scores, or editorials. (Nor do I suggest that you read the classifieds like poetry.) Just like some of my students who confess they don't like poetry, I suspect that many of us don't read much poetry at all. Learning to read the Psalms (not to mention the Old Testament Wisdom Literature and the Prophets) requires that we try.

One useful approach is to learn something about how the structure of the poetry works, just as in a literature class we might learn about rhyme, rhythm, and the stress pattern in iambic pentameter. Many people find the Psalms more accessible when they know how the repetition and development of ideas grows out of the Hebrew poetic principle of parallelism. It's an interesting and useful pursuit, and those who understand it can better read the Psalms both for artfulness and accuracy. Structural understandings alone, however, won't unpack Hebrew poetry any more than mastering iambic pentameter will reveal the treasures in William Shakespeare's sonnets.

Poetry, including the Psalms, invites us to read with our imaginations and our hearts. The language is vivid, visual, sensate. It is filled with stirring images and, in the Psalms particularly, with high exaggeration (or hyperbole). It is trying to crack open places of complacent thinking, to jolt lethargic hearts. It stretches to say things we can hardly speak of, to point to the mysteries we know are true but don't have the words for. To read the Psalms well, we must learn to listen on these terms, for there are some things that we can know only by heart.

It helps me to think of reading visually, that is, reading slowly and attentively enough to let pictures unfold and to savor them. Many of the word pictures are right at hand because they come from nature. We can recall seeing dry, cracked ground thirsting for rain. We can imagine timely, abundant rain making the earth glad. When I get to hear the crashing waves of the ocean, I can imagine it roaring its joy in God's rule, and with it forests and hills singing and rivers clapping their hands. In my mind I can feel the shelter of strong walls or high mountain caves, the comforting provision of green pastures and gentle waters.

The language of hyperbole invites us to enter more with the heart than with reason. The singer's awareness of sin leads him to say that his iniquities are "more than the hairs of my head" (Psalm 40:12) or that he was a sinner even from conception, a wicked zygote (Psalms 51:5). This is not the language of definition and proof texts, as it is often taken. Nor is the witness that God removes our transgression "as far as the east is from the west" (Psalm 103:12) or the confession (or complaint?) that we can't escape God's presence—from the heavens to Sheol, east to west, in the darkness (Psalm 139). This is the language of high exaggeration that points beyond itself to even greater realities.

Reading the Psalms in this way requires patience, waiting, a receptive imagination. Sometimes we can act to grow our imaginations a bit, perhaps by experimenting with vivid language of our own in response to the Psalms or by being more attentive to our experience, or by sharing the experience and vision of others. I like illustrated "coffee-table" books to help with this, particularly those that picture the land and living culture of those who first sang these songs. In any event, we can act purposefully to receive the poetry of the Psalms and let it blow the doors off our hearts and minds and open us to new worlds of knowing God.

Praying the Psalms

In *Answering God*, Eugene Peterson insists that we can come to know the Psalms only by praying them. The more I use the Psalms, the more I agree with him. For one thing, as he teaches, the language of the Psalms is the language of intimacy and relationship, not the language of description or information. To understand the language of encounter, we must enter and embrace it, not stand outside it. We best understand the language of adoration and confession, despair and doubt, thanksgiving and trust when we share it rather than when we observe it.

I have already observed that in praying the Psalms God teaches us to pray, opening the themes and language of prayer. Yet, as we enter them, the Psalms do more than give us the language we need. They also become a mirror, revealing obscure or hidden realities about who we are, how we live our lives, and how we respond to God. As we enter into the language of relationship, God uses them to search us out, to challenge, to comfort and to renew. This is one of the reasons that Peterson, Martin Luther, Dietrich Bonhoeffer, and the historic practice of the Church in the daily office and the lectionary insist that we need to pray all of the Psalms, even the ones that seem difficult for us.

The Quaker insistence on integrity, which I heartily share, rejected early on using prayers from government-approved prayer books, honoring instead prayer prompted directly by God. I remember well, in what I now regard as youthful arrogance, inwardly judging a minister who used a prayer book to lead in public prayer. The poor guy, in my mind an impostor of sorts, surely didn't know God well enough to really pray. In my experience, sometimes overly earnest worship leaders, urging me to pay attention to the words of songs and sing them like I really mean it, have heightened the question of integrity. Yet using the Psalms, all of them, does not violate this concern. Other Christians who, like Friends, rejected the prayer books, never abandoned the Psalms. Indeed, for some of them, these were, and are even now, the only songs they would sing in worship. They knew that entering into the Psalms is a way of being present to God, expectant and vulnerable, as well as a way of being fully part of God's people.

One approach to the Psalms I find helpful is meditation on scripture or *lectio divina*, "holy reading." Guides to this ancient practice describe it helpfully in a variety of ways, though at its heart it is quite simple. It is reading patiently, attentively, expecting that God may encounter us and teach us through the text. As we read, a word or phrase may particularly grab our attention; guides will refer to this variously as a warming, a stop, an almost visual lighting, a sizzle. Whatever that bump may be, it invites us to wait there, to brood over and savor the text, to wait to see how this may be an opening to God's moving in us. When feeling released from that place, we can read on or, depending on our leading, conclude in a way appropriate to that experience.

A similarly helpful approach is to pray the scripture. At one level, of course, we enter into the words of the psalm, which is a prayer, and we use those words to express our own heart, to guide us in prayer. But we can go beyond that by taking the words of the psalm and expanding them, letting them guide us as we offer our own hearts to God in praise, in pain, in confusion, in neediness, in deep gladness, wherever we may be. It's another way of letting God help our prayer as well as hear our prayer.

Two other particular practices help me enter the Psalms in prayer and worship. The first is simply reading the Psalms aloud. It engages more fully our senses and energies—seeing, speaking, hearing, making choices in interpreting—in ways that are surprisingly helpful. The second is to sing the Psalms. After all, they are songs, and the coupling of lyric and melody is very powerful. We largely guess about what the original musical forms might have been, but the Psalms have gathered many musical settings over the years from chant to chorale to jazz. Using those that reach us individually can open new insights and deepen the Psalms' transforming power in our lives.

Finally, I've become increasingly aware that we sing and pray the Psalms in the context of the community of faith. At one level I know that these songs come to me from the "blessed fellowship" or "communion of saints," from the people of God who first wrote and sang them and the people who have cherished them through many centuries. I am also moved to know that in any moment I read, pray, and sing the Psalms, I am joining countless others around the world, in many places and many conditions, who are sharing the same songs. We sing with each other. But, in our local fellowships and in solidarity with the people of God around the world, we may also sing on behalf of one another.

For any of us at any given moment, not every psalm speaks to our circumstances. We may not resonate with words of praise, or of thanksgiving, or of complaint, or of pleas to be delivered from persecutors. At any moment, however, each psalm speaks directly to some in the larger fellowship. So we can sing each other's songs in the spirit of rejoicing with those who rejoice and weeping with those who weep. As we enter in, the Psalms may alert us to the condition of others, tendering our hearts and inviting our care. We can sing songs gladly in support of others, and sometimes on behalf of others who are in such straits that they cannot even sing for themselves.

The Psalms are an inexhaustible treasure. Though I've studied and taught them often, they still invite me to understand them more thoughtfully, receive them more imaginatively and enter them more prayerfully. My journey has just begun.

Bibliography

Peterson, Eugene. *Answering God: The Psalms as Tools for Prayer*. San Francisco: HarperCollins, 1989.

Manuel Guzman-Martínez, a Mexican Friend, studied at the Instituto Evangélistico de México where he earned his degree in Pastoral Studies. He served as Pastor of Ciudad Victoria Monthly Meeting from 1984 until 1999, with breaks in 1988-89 to study at Pendle Hill in Wallingford, Pennsylvania and in 1993-96 to earn a Master of Divinity degree from the Earlham School of Religion in Richmond, Indiana. For several years he has travelled in the ministry in Latin America under the sponsorship of the Friends World Committee for Consultation. He is proud of being identified as a Quaker.

Manuel is a poet, although he writes only when inspired to do so.

READINGS ON THE BOOK OF ECCLESIASTES

Manuel Guzman-Martínez

When I got the invitation to write an article regarding how I, as a Quaker, read a biblical text, I was excited and thought that writing that article would be so easy and would flow with no difficulty. I consulted with the editors on which book of the Bible to write about and, after some considerations and thought, I chose the book of Ecclesiastes.

The first thing I did was to read the book many times. Then I took some notes and organized an outline, but in the process of writing I became blocked. I thought since my mind was full of ideas, the writing would not be a real problem. Involved as I am in my every day activities, I postponed writing and it became a burden to me. I told a friend about it and she encouraged me to just try to write. She said: "You are sure you know what you want to write about; so just do it." It might seem unbelievable, but those words inspired me and I began writing. In the process, the original outline disappeared. I had the impression that the book could be read and explained by following a thought, but I discovered, that it had to be read as if the reader—me—were in a labyrinth. That is to say, that the writer insistently repeats his ideas with different words and with the echoes of haunting phrases to make his point clear.

Observations

It is believed by many scholars that the book of Ecclesiastes was written by King Solomon. My first observation was that Solomon's discourse in the book sounds too pessimistic. We live in situations where hope and optimism must occupy the first seats in the auditorium of the world, but reading the words of this writer made me think that hope and optimism are sent to occupy the last seats. However, I realized that the last seats give a wider and bigger perspective on what is happening. It is my opinion that, even though some of the words of Ecclesiastes may sound pessimistic, if the book is read carefully the reader might find a suitable and right interpretation for himself or herself. In this text, real things that happen in real life are said without fear of hurting anybody's feelings. In the long run, it is better to know the truth no matter how hurtful it may be—to know that deception and hypocrisy have had dominion over us and we have been living in deceit.

A second observation was how different my reading was now, from readings I had done when I was young. I am middle-aged. Re-reading the book helped me to comprehend how much I identified with the writer as a person who has had many experiences in life and recorded them. Of course, I am not a wealthy man nor have I had one thousand wives as he did. Nor have I had hundreds if not thousands of servants, but I have passed through the years of my life observing and keeping a record of my observations as he did, so my observations are as important as his.

When I was young, I read the book without comprehending it. Maybe because I was young and the perspective of the writer was of somebody old. Young people have a hard time understanding old fellows. In that time, I did not understand that I had to live life in order to know it, so I restrained myself from having some experiences in life. My reading of the book indicated to me that in order to be close to God I had to avoid to live some things. My last readings before writing this article stirred old memories, telling me I had God so close in my life, but that I had forgotten to experience the beautiful world in which God put me to live. Experience teaches us many things, unfortunately sometimes it arrives late. The paradox and dilemma is that by living close to God we restrain ourselves from having some experiences. The writer experienced many things and he writes to advise people to avoid making the mistakes he made. Unfortunately, no one learns in someone else's shoes. What a fortunate thing it would be if young people followed the advice of older people and avoided committing the mistakes they made.

I entitled this article "Readings on the Book of Ecclesiastes" because I wanted to talk about in detail on how I read the Bible, and especially how I read this book, from 10 possible perspectives—then I had to narrow it down even further to only five. Each reading is different, although I know that each aspect plays an important part in my interpretation of the book.

First Reading: The Book of Ecclesiastes as a Unity

In my first reading on the book of Ecclesiastes, I discovered that its main topic is life and its subtopics are experience, work, and wisdom. In my opinion, the writer's perspective is too fatalist, he asserts that all in life is vanity. Over and over he states: "Vanity of vanities, all is vanity" (1:2). He also says that his experience in life—based on all that he did—is important in proving that truth.

Solomon was king of Jerusalem; he had everything that a human being could have aspired to have. He declares: "I became great and surpassed all who were before me in Jerusalem" (2:9). From this, it can be inferred that he worked hard. This is a man who decided to write about the meaning of life based on his experiences and hard work. He was a man who was not lazy at all—a hard worker who had more riches and possessions than anyone could use in a lifetime. So, his opinions come from a wealthy person who had everything, nevertheless, he writes with a pessimistic tone.

This makes Ecclesiastes a difficult book to read, but it has a unifying message. It starts with the idea that life is cyclical, which means there is repetition in every event that occurs. Every single person, no matter what gender, age, status, or race, is involved in that recurrence of events. Human beings cannot control events in life. These happen one after another, the good ones and the bad ones. That dualism allows people to discover that the world in which they live is dual, and therefore, permits them to experience opposite feelings as happiness and sadness.

It is obvious to me that the difficulty of the book continues from beginning to end, keeping its same tone, though. I deduce from the book that if human beings choose the side of riches and possessions, in the end they will be disappointed because material things offer no satisfaction when the time to depart this world approaches. And, the haunting words remind the readers that, with no exception every man and woman, old or young, rich or poor, black or white, all will die. So, life for Solomon makes no sense at all. As we arrive, we will depart. In that, there is a sense of nothingness. Those who keep in mind that life is temporary are rewarded with a happy farewell. It seems that all the days of our existence must be dedicated to dignifying our departure from this world.

Later, a new element is included in this picture, which causes the tone of the book to change a little, giving hope. Its name is wisdom. Wisdom makes all the difference in the ways in which human beings live their lives. It is a matter of making decisions, of making the right choices. The fates of those who make wrong decisions and those who make right decisions might appear to be the same, but they are not. Those who make the wrong decision can never articulate the meaning of their lives, while the ones who make the right decision can explain each step of the way with clarity, satisfaction, and pride. Their fates might seem the same, but the way in which they are articulated makes all the difference. In short, I read Ecclesiastes following the dynamic of disentangling the puzzle that life entails. Work and experience, experience and work, but above all wisdom, which makes the difference. In closure to this reading, the reflective reader is advised to recognize God as the one to be remembered and, in so doing, honoured.

Second Reading: Questioning Everything

The book of Ecclesiastes is too dense to be read without asking questions. This enables us to understand, little-by-little, the meaning of what the author tried to convey. We must read as if we were having a conversation with the author. When I converse with friends and I do not understand exactly what they are saying, I am forced to ask them questions to clarify what I do not understand and to put my ideas together. Similarly, an adequate strategy for understanding a text is to isolate the most intriguing ideas and seek out their meaning. In other words, to read the text as if I were talking with someone, but only asking the most pertinent questions to avoid disrupting the flow of conversation. I stop and ask questions only when it is impossible to continue reading. For instance, at 1:18 I interrupted my reading for what the author says: "For in much wisdom is much vexation, and those who increase knowledge increase sorrow." To me, it seems paradoxical to suggest a knowledgeable person will suffer because of his or her knowledge. I asked myself: Is that possible? But immediately I came to understand that the writer, in his vast experience, thought that he was responsible for what he knew.

Continuing with my reading I discovered that the writer laments his hard work saying: "I hated all my toil in which I had toiled under the sun, seeing that I must leave it to those who come after me... What do mortals get from all the toil and strain with which they toil under the sun?" (2:18, 22). Everything is the repetition of a story that has been lived by others, is lived by ourselves, and will be lived by still others to come again. Life experiences are one and the same. As human beings, the stories of our lives are too predictable that no matter what we do, we repeat what others did. This is when I ask the text: Why does the writer lament all the hard work he had done? Why does he say that it was without consequence? Is it that he sees the future as a time when others who had not worked, would benefit from his deeds?

I think that out of his experience, the writer speaks his mind. The words echo and resonate as he poses the question: "What gain have the workers from their toil?" (3:9). His insistence makes me consider that perhaps he was not fully convinced of the cyclical nature of the activities in which human beings are inevitably involved.

To me it is interesting to notice that I am not the only one asking questions; the author is, too. With the discourse centered on the material aspects of life, the writer introduces the topic of life after death. This gives place to the inference that the material aspects of life are just that. He asks; "Who knows whether the human spirit goes upward and the spirit of animals goes downward to the earth?" (3:21). The question is rhetorical, and the answer is obvious: nobody knows. The writer uses this linguistic method to indicate that he does not know there is life after life; we have to accept that one of these two lives we know; the other we may perceive to exist, but we can not prove it. Life after life is perceived to exist, though.

The writer uses the following words when he talks about life as we know it: "As they came from their mother's womb, so they shall go again, naked as they came; they shall take nothing for their toil, which they may carry away with their hands" (5:15). I think that this tragic truth, questioning the value of life as we know it, needs to be addressed. If there is some value in life, what is it? What is the advantage of working hard to have lots of riches, if in the end we are all the same, with the same possessions: nothing? What is the advantage of being wiser than others if, at the end of our lives, our knowledge will guarantee nothing? These questions lead us to no answers; the future is uncertain and dubious.

It is my belief that all the experiences we have in life— for good or bad—are part of ourselves as persons. They give us a position, a perspective, a place to stand when we face the possibility of another life. In fact, the writer sees death as better than life itself. He says: "A good name is better than precious ointment, and the day of death, than the day of birth... Better is the end of a thing than its beginning" (7:1,8). Toil and work and experience are treated as if they were only the departed's preparation for another life. Therefore I ask again, is the life we know the introduction to a life yet to be known and lived? If so, how to be better prepared?

In another part of the text, the author juxtaposes good people who die with evildoers who prolong their evil existences: "In my vain life I have seen everything; there are righteous people who perish in their righteousness, and there are wicked people who prolong their life in their evildoing" (7:15). To me, this raises the question of justice.

How is it possible to judge good and evil? How is it possible for bad people to live longer than good people? How come? Their lives are destructive, pernicious, and hurtful. I have not found a simple answer to this question. Perhaps an answer could be drawn by imagining different parameters to measure justice—parameters that the naked eye cannot see nor the ear hear, but that live within the hearts of people who feel their own judgement, and have themselves as their own best judges.

Still talking about justice, people sometimes do not receive the judgement they deserve. The author calls this, vanity: "There is a vanity that takes place on earth, that there are righteous people who are treated according to the conduct of the wicked, and there are wicked people who are treated according to the conduct of the righteous. I said that this also is vanity" (8:14). The author is simply pointing out a fact—something that happens repeatedly on earth. The previous words lead me to ask: Why does such injustice happen? The writer insists and advises us to enjoy life as a compensation for the hard times we live: "So I commend enjoyment, for there is nothing better for people under the sun than to eat, and drink, and enjoy themselves, for this will go with them in their toil through the days of life that God gives them under the sun" (8:15).

Taking for granted that injustice exists, the writer separates people into two categories, the wise and the foolish, and encourages them to search for wisdom even if it is based on the judgement of others. On the other hand, the author justifies the fact that people can "enjoy themselves" because this is what they will take with them when they die. These words make me ask again: How can a person live his or her life looking for wisdom while at the same time enjoying life? Isn't the search for wisdom and the kind of conduct that leads to wisdom incongruent with such enjoyment?

The writer declares in advance that the search for wisdom does not matter because, in the end, it is going to be fruitless. Human beings die. "The living know that they will die, but the dead know nothing; they have no more reward, and even the memory of them is lost" (9:5). To me, if the only true knowledge is the certainty of death, then once we know that, we know the ultimate. Anyone can attain that knowledge. Many of us come to know that the only certain thing in this life is death. The sequence of this argumentation makes me ask: What then are we to live for?

After these thoughts about life in "this world," the writer turns to the place where human beings are going to go—a place he called "Sheol." We are told to live life as fully as possible before death. "Whatever your hand finds to do, do with your might; for there is no work or thought or knowledge or wisdom in Sheol, to which you are going" (9:10). With this new element of a place to go after death and knowing that the end of each mortal being is death I question again: What are human beings supposed to do on this earth?

Once we have clear in the text that we as human beings have the same end, the element of wisdom distinguishes who is who in this earth. In his discourse, the author describes the different ways that fools and wise people act. He clearly favours the wise exercising authority and conducting the government. "Happy are you, O land, when your king is a nobleman, and your princes feast at the proper time—for strength, and not for drunkenness!" (10:17). Even though we all share a final fate, wisdom makes the difference between a good life and a wicked one.

Up to this point, we have read about our own judgement and others' judgements. Almost at the end of the book, the author turns to God's judgment, writing: "Rejoice, young man, while you are young, and let your heart cheer you in the days of your youth. Follow the inclination of your heart and the desire of your eyes, but know that for all these things God will bring you into judgment" (11:9). I think God's judgement is presented as an exhortation to consider, and not as a warning to condemn. The writer in the last chapter of Ecclesiastes draws an analogy to the physical body of a man or woman which, through the passing of time, deteriorates. Those who become old are the ones who analyze everything, because they feel their departure from this world is near. In closing his treatise, the writer declares his purpose in writing this book saying: "The sayings of the wise are like goads, and like nails firmly fixed are the collected sayings that are given by one shepherd. Of anything beyond these, my child, beware. Of making many books there is no end, and much study is a weariness of the flesh. The end of the matter; all has been heard. Fear God, and keep his commandments; for that is the whole duty of everyone. For God will bring every deed into judgment, including every secret thing, whether good or evil" (12:11-14). In my opinion, Solomon changes drastically his tone and in few lines—compared with the rest of his writing—lets the readers see hope sneaking silently into the scene of all this pessimistic noise of vanity and futility.

Third Reading: Immediate Reactions for Further Analysis

Many of the ideas developed in this book generate immediate reactions in the reader. Further consideration and careful analysis of such ideas will bring more thoughtful opinions.

One of the writer's first conclusions is about the sameness of all the episodes of a life. He writes this way: "What has been is what will be, and what has been done is what will be done; there is nothing new under the sun" (1:9). He considers the immense opportunities he enjoyed as king of Jerusalem. He writes that: "Whatever my eyes desired I did not keep from them; I kept my heart from no pleasure, for my heart found pleasure in all my toil, and this was my reward for all my toil" (2:10). As we see, the writer experienced all that was available for him to do and found pleasure in doing it. An immediate reaction for me was that the writer was like an empirical researcher who found in the concept of pleasure one of most the important elements in his investigations.

He says that pleasure is an important measure on how a life is rated. I reacted to this with disbelief. In verses 2:23-24 the writer states: "For all their days are full of pain, and their work is a vexation; even at night their minds do not rest. This also is vanity. There is nothing better for mortals than to eat and drink, and find enjoyment in their toil." Verse 23 refers to the pain which characterizes life, but if life is surrounded by pain, the only way in which that pain can be mitigated is through its counterpart referred to in the second verse—the enjoyments in life. Pleasure with no limits nor boundaries to balance a fatiguing life of work and toil. To me, the words in the above verses are too general and therefore give excuse to live disorderly.

Still another conclusion to be analyzed without pressure of time comes in verse 3:11 "He has made everything suitable for its time; moreover he has put a sense of past and future into their minds, yet they cannot find out what God has done from the beginning to the end." I react to these words giving God the image of a sovereign who does whatever God pleases to do. In those verses, God has designed the way life must be. On the other hand, some verses ahead the writer affirms: "For the fate of humans and the fate of animals is the same; as one dies, so dies the other. They all have the same breath, and humans have no advantage over the animals; for all is vanity" (3:19). Just as God designed life, God has also designed death. My reaction puts me in mind of the alternative—to wonder to what extent God decides and to what extent human beings also decide.

Continuing with my reading, I found other interesting verses in which I deduced something for further analysis, as the writer insists in 4:1, "Again I saw all the oppressions that are practiced under the sun. Look, the tears of the oppressed—with no one to comfort them! On the side of their oppressors there was power—with no one to comfort them." My first thought was that we have a twofold world with good people and bad people. The good people in the world have no consolation due to the oppression of the bad people, while the oppressors have no consolation since the injustice they practice lets them have no peace of mind. My second thought was still the same, what a tragic scene is this world! Full of people working to discover reasons to live with others obstructing the efforts and desires of good people. Human beings have two options in life to choose between: good or bad. After that comes death. And what is after that? "For who knows what is good for mortals while they live the few days of their vain life, which they pass like a shadow? For who can tell them what will be after them under the sun?" (6:12). The writer has analyzed everything through the empiric knowledge of observations and experience, but he has no evidence from which to say what comes after life. Nevertheless, perhaps based on the tragic and fatalist picture of life he has shown, he is sure that unknown death is better than life. "A good name is better than precious ointment, and the day of death, than the day of birth" (7:1). In short, the reading does not give enough room to have definite conclusions, but I recognize in it someone who tried to be a successful researcher; I discovered that God is presented by the researcher as a sovereign being; and that the result of his observations pointed to a two-sided world with good and evil, finally the issue of death is explored with no final conclusions.

Fourth Reading: Allowing My Emotions to Get Involved in the Reading

One of the first things I felt when I read this book was interest. The wisdom literature, considered as literature of advice through ancient sayings—to which Ecclesiastes belongs—is captivating, like hearing the words of a wise man. And like a good story, wisdom literature can be listened to hundreds of times without losing its freshness. Therefore, each time I read the book, I felt an enormous desire to learn and appreciate its words from a new perspective. I was drawn in by the developing themes as they guided me into new ideas, new conclusions, and new interpretations.

Another emotion I had in my reading was perplexity. The apparent contradictions of the text led me to feel as if I had been in a puzzle—good and evil fight each other, each seeking to prevail and each having a part in the lives of all human beings. The unfairness of life was and is one of the aspects that made me feel this way.

Perplexity does not come alone, it is accompanied by frustration. How can I not be upset and sick about things that are not supposed to happen? How can I not oppose all the political, social, cultural, and religious injustices revealed?

Reading Ecclesiastes also made me feel incapable of finding answers about the meaning of life. Many questions were proposed and remain unanswered—particularly those regarding birth, death, and the other life. Reading the book evokes the existential questions: Where do I come from? Why am I here? Where will I go? But if the writer was a researcher of life, he left the implications of his investigations to be followed by other researchers because there is no final and definite conclusion. And reading the book made me feel like a researcher who, in moving closer to finding meaning to his life, finds himself further at the end of the investigation.

How can I not allow my emotions to be present when I read the arguments and revelations of a person inspired by

God to disclose hidden truths in such a subtle manner? Permitting my emotions to emerge brought the text closer to me. My emotions enhanced the understanding I have of the text and allowed me to be honest with myself, with the author in his time and his perspective, and with God. As I mentioned, perplexity and frustration were some of the feelings I had while reading the text. This does not mean that these feelings were the only ones I had when I read the text. These were the feelings that I named, but some other unmentioned feelings also appeared. I suppose that what I am trying to say is that the respect I have for the text does not impede me from showing myself as I am: naked to the light of the sacred text, looking in introspection to know me better. So the interest for the book remains untouched, the perplexity to understand paradoxical truths also remains untouched, while the frustration in not finding answers tends to be lightened by the hope that something good must be behind the veil of untouchable matters.

Fifth Reading: Applying the Text to My Life

The contextualization of the text is the most difficult part of the process of reading. It is my conviction that people tend to use the first person plural "we" instead of using the first singular person "I" in order to hide in the anonymous multitude and not confront "myself" with the text. I believe the scriptures are part of the divine revelation of God. I also believe that it is my responsibility to discern how a particular text speaks to me.

It is clear that the times, cultures, customs, traditions, and many more things are different now than when the book was originally written. Evidently the meaning of the text to readers in its time was also different from the meaning it has for me now. However, I recognize an appropriateness to me in the text. It is never so old that it cannot still speak with truth. It is never so distant that it will not let me approach it. It is never so complex that I cannot decipher it. It is never so unintelligible that I cannot find translations. The text is so generous that it accepts all kinds of interpretations, so long as these are rooted in piety. What does that mean? It means that if I have good intentions when I read the text, my conclusions will not be manipulative, oppressive, or self-directed to achieve material benefits. On the other hand, if my intentions are selfish, then the text will be distorted, causing hurt to other people.

God is always present with me and the text— transcending all these barriers of language, styles of writing, translations, idiomatic expressions, culture, and history. Reading it requires an open mind to assess how what was useful, and has been useful, for others can still serve as a tool to disclose God's revelation to me.

The confrontation between the text and me sometimes is upsetting due to my human resistance to accepting that I have committed wrong things in my life. However, the never ending dialogue with the text has positive results in convincing me to modify my personal perspectives and, in the long run, my life.

Through biblical texts, God provides me with good things. Reading a biblical text imprints in me eternal words. These become so much a part of me that I will always remember them. For example, as I mentioned before, the writer says in 1:18, "For in much wisdom is much vexation, and those who increase knowledge increase sorrow." These words have become part of me as a person who inquires, argues, confronts others with ideas, fights with his arguments, but almost always recognizes the right of others to think differently. The application of this particular verse to my life attracts me to know more, but puts me in peril—the more I know, the more responsible I must be to do or not to do what my knowledge tells me.

On an everyday basis, many people discuss quite a good number of different subjects with me. A lot of times, to know something has given me sorrow. To really apply the text to my world here and now, the embodiment of that knowledge requires changes in my attitude, behavior, and service. In consequence, if I put my life in the right context, I will allow that confrontation. The only way to do that is to read as if someone were speaking to me, and I were listening.

At the end of this exercise of discipline—of reading Ecclesiastes—I found that as a reader, with God as the transmitter and receiver in this communication, my good intentions to look for what is good for me, and the confrontation I have had with the text have not yet produced a change in attitude or effort to do some things differently from the way I did them. I am a person who works as most people do, but I have not put work as an ultimate purpose in my existence. I dedicated most of the years of my life to God's service, but now I am giving myself permission to live as I did not live when I was one hundred percent involved in what I called my ministry.

This situation creates a tension between the good man that I was and the investigator that I am now. Reading this text has made me think of redoing the things I did, letting my inquiries of experiencing life aside, because with what I did I was satisfied while with what I do now I have an empty space in my life that needs to be filled with the exhortation to fear God.

Reflection

There are many ways to read a biblical text. There are many readers. Some of them are scholars and others are non-scholars. All the readings—from the most knowledgeable to the less knowledgeable—are valid if (and only if) they are done honestly.

What does that mean? It means that my reading cannot be done to prove I am right in my own opinions. It means I cannot say something that is not said in the text. It means I might be in agreement with the text or not. It means each reading is a new one, no matter how many times I had read the text before. It means each time I have new possibilities to see the unseen or not revealed.

As I have said before, I read Ecclesiastes many times in order to write this article. I had read it many times before as part of my formation as a pastor and with some degree of expertise on biblical texts. The opinions I had of the book of Ecclesiastes then were probably not too different from the ones I have now, but the perspectives are. It is not the same to read Ecclesiastes as an adolescent and to read it as a middle-aged person. The book is the same, the person, "me," is the same to some degree and in others not, but the encounter with the expressed truths does not change. Man ("me") and text ("God's words") are interwoven to create a magnificent piece of work from the hand of God. Together, this new creation makes sense out of nonsense, finds understanding where there was no communication, gives life in the agony of our difficult times in which "we" seem to be dying every day. The blessed words move constantly and in all directions; they invade everywhere to state what needs to be stated, and to name what needs to be named in a world where the unwise try to make us think that the mumbling lies prevail.

Let us follow the words of wisdom that guide us to the eternal. Amen.

Dave Phillips was born in Marion, Indiana and raised on a farm near Jonesboro, Indiana, where he attended the Jonesboro Friends Church. He graduated from Taylor University in 1967. He has studied at Columbia International University in South Carolina, Anderson School of Theology, Grace Theological Seminary, and Fuller Seminary. Since 1975, he has pastored in Indiana Yearly Meeting, at the Farmland Friends Church from 1971-75 and at the Wabash Friends Church ever since.

Though Dave and Debbie were reared 30 miles apart in Indiana, they met in New York City working in a camp for inner city children. Their love blossomed and grew. They were married in 1968. Their son Michael and his wife Natalie live in Apple Valley, California with their two children Jedediah and Carolina. He likes to read, walk, garden, and travel.

THE WORD THAT SUSTAINS THE WEARY

David Phillips

My Personal Journey with the Bible

From the time I was a baby, my parents took me to the Jonesboro Friends Church every Sunday. Sunday School class was a part of that routine. I remember dedicated women teaching me Bible stories. When I was nine years old, my parents purchased a set of books. Part of this set was several volumes that contained Bible stories from Genesis to Revelation. I read this through in one summer.

When I was eleven, I gave my life to Christ at Quaker Haven camp. I knew I needed to read the Bible, but it was difficult to understand. I gave up on personal study until I took a deeper step of commitment to Christ in my senior year of high school. This hunger to know and understand the Bible increased while I was a student in college. It intensified while teaching elementary school after college. When my fellow teachers discovered I was a Christian, they asked me questions about the Bible I could not answer. I read the Bible through that year. Questions began to emerge: How does one study the Bible? Why are their so many interpretations of scripture? Can you make the Bible say whatever you want it to? How does one explain or defend the Bible? How can one know truth?

I knew that if I was to grow spiritually, I had to get a better handle on the Bible and how to study it, so I quit teaching and enrolled in a graduate program at Columbia

Bible College (now Columbia International University) in Columbia, South Carolina from 1968 to 1971. I purposely chose one that was not Quaker and had a cross-cultural emphasis. I lived, worked, and studied in three hot beds of learning during the civil rights and anti-war movements— a housing project that had just been integrated, a graduate library at a major university, and a graduate school dedicated to developing workers in cross-cultural ministry.

I led the youth group and taught a class of children in the little, integrated church in the project. How does one teach the Bible in the midst of poverty and prejudice? I supervised students on my shift in the graduate library. How does one share his or her faith in a fairly hostile environment? I even went through a time of doubting the Bible. It was during this time I became fully convinced of the Bible's authority and trustworthiness. This has been confirmed over the years in seeking spiritual growth, in ministering, in counseling, and in teaching.

Out of an intense time of physical, emotional, and spiritual suffering in my third year of study, I sensed the call to pastor. My wife had become ill with what they thought was multiple sclerosis; our son developed asthma; and I came down with a severe case of mononucleosis. I had to take several weeks off work and had to drop out of school. I was in bed for most of six weeks. It seemed like everything God had led me to do was falling apart. The discouragement and depression were very intense. It was all darkness. I had thoughts I thought I would never think. Previously I used to run several miles for fun, now I could not walk more than ten yards without exhaustion. I'd had a positive, goal-centered, "can do anything" attitude. Now I could do nothing but wait.

When I first enrolled, being a pastor was the last thing on my mind. I had planned to return to teaching. I took no courses to be a pastor. All my classes centered on the Bible, church history, psychology, and anthropology. The 1960s were not kind to churches, but one of my professors in the Philosophy of Missions class made the statement: "The local church is still God's primary way to reach the world." I wrestled with that principle during this time of darkness. Out of this time, the call to be pastor began to emerge. It was with reluctance, and yet with anticipation, that I began to seek God's will for a pastorate. It was clear it was to be among Friends. Part of that call was to learn to teach the Bible so that people would understand who God in Christ is, and so they would be transformed to reach out to others. Little did I know it would be in my home yearly meeting.

The Bible's Place in Personal and Corporate Spiritual Growth

In my own relationship with Jesus, the Bible is very vital. I find that if I do not consistently read, study, meditate, and pray through scripture, I literally cannot survive. These have moved from spiritual disciplines in my life to absolute necessities. I read through the Bible one to three times a year, using different translations. I underline verses that are meaningful and date the chapters read to keep my place. Memorization is more difficult now, but I try to stay immersed in the word. One of my life purpose statements is "To master the Bible to be able to apply it to every life situation." I encourage others to develop a program or discipline that enables them to stay in scripture, not just to learn facts, but to understand God and his purposes for us in Christ and to be transformed into the image of Christ.

The body of Christ needs to be fed. It is a spiritual body needing spiritual food. The Bible is a primary source the Holy Spirit uses to feed our spirit. The written Word informs us of the living Word. Jesus' words feed our soul. For Christ's body to grow, the Bible needs to be a part of our worship together, our study together, our life together, and our service together. People with the gift of teaching need to be nurtured and encouraged in our meetings to develop and use this gift. Teaching is a primary function of leadership in a local meeting. I want to live and teach the Bible in such a way to feed God's people a healthy, balanced diet that strengthens, edifies, and produces fruit for the kingdom. I desire that people learn to read and study the Bible in a way to feed themselves.

Using the Bible in Spiritual Growth and Ministry

The following are practical steps and principles that help me understand the message God gave to the writers so we can more accurately apply it to our lives today. These principles are so much a part of my life now that I do them almost automatically. You may want to write them down in your Bible to review before you start reading.

Ask the Holy Spirit to teach and to help you understand what the scripture says

The author of any book is the best source to understand the contents of the book. The Holy Spirit is the author of the Bible. He moved in the hearts and minds of the writers over a period of around fifteen hundred years to give us an accurate account of what happened and to tell us the message God wants us to receive. The intellect alone is not enough; one needs the Spirit to teach us. The great leaders in the Quaker movement possessed both a keen mind and a dependency on the Holy Spirit. Often I find myself praying over a text: "O Lord, by your Spirit give understanding of your word. May I see clearly what I need to understand for myself and for those you have given me to minister and teach."

Learn to see the Bible as a whole

The Bible is not just a collection of books thrown together over time by the whim of men. There is a historical and thematic thread running through the whole book. As one college student told me after he read the Bible through for the first time, it all fit together. The thread that runs through Genesis to Revelation is redemption.

One possible outline of the Bible as a whole is:

The Need for Redemption—Genesis 1-11

The Channel of Redemption—Genesis 12-Malachi

The Purchase of Redemption—Matthew—John

The Proclamation of Redemption—Acts

The Explanation of Redemption—Romans—Jude

The Consummation of Redemption—Revelation

There are other useful outlines that can help you to see the Bible as a whole. Mortimer Adler's *How to Read a Book* was helpful to me in this process. When I study a portion of scripture, I seek to see where it fits in this historical thread. How does it fit into the big picture God is painting in His word?

Know what you can about the writer

I try to see how the writer's experience and situation affect his writings. The more I can know about the writer, the easier it is to interpret what he says. For example, Isaiah was close to the kings of Judah. He was an adviser to Hezekiah. He is found in the history books giving aid and counsel to Hezekiah. His call to be a prophet is found in the well-known sixth chapter of Isaiah. His ministry covered a relatively long period of time.

Take the language seriously

The Bible was written in human languages. Hebrew, Aramaic, and Koine Greek are the languages in which the original text was written. This is because these were the common languages of the times in which it was written. For many years, linguists and Bible scholars have been working on various paraphrases and translations to make the language relevant to the readers of the day. When one reads and studies the Bible, it is important to understand how to interpret figures of speech and various literary devices. I have to work hard to understand the figures of speech a writer uses. Biblical writers especially use metaphor and simile. Dr. J. Robert Clinton's book *Having a Ministry that Lasts: Becoming a Bible Centered Leader* was helpful in this and other practical aspects of coming to understand the Bible. There are many others as well that can be helpful.

One teacher I studied under compared this process to a railroad track. For the train to move forward and not derail, the two rails had to be parallel. If one deviated too far in either direction, the train would wreck. The two rails for staying on track in understanding the Bible are the laws of the Spirit and the laws of language. This has helped me understand why people can come up with different interpretations of the same text—it is difficult to keep a balance. If one over emphasized the rail of the Spirit, he or she can be more mystical than the text allows. The early church father Origen did this. His commentary often can leave the reader wondering where his ideas came from and how they relate to the text. It can sound very "spiritual," but it can easily lead the reader astray. I remember times as a youth listening to speakers and wondering where they were coming from. An overbalance on this rail can lead to "mushy" thinking and error. It can lead to a disregard for the moral and ethical teaching of scripture.

An over-emphasis on the language rail can lead to a harsh understanding of scripture. People start fighting over every jot and tittle of the text. Studying the Bible becomes a purely intellectual exercise that can lead to cold and impersonal interpretations. Legalism often comes from this approach. This is similar to what Elton Trueblood used to say, that Christians need to be tough minded but tenderhearted. I work hard in seeking the Spirit to teach and in understanding the language.

Robertson McQuilkin's book *Understanding and Applying the Bible* is helpful in a beginning study.

Interpret in the context of the time written

What was the writer trying to communicate to the reader? How would a reader or hearer have understood the author or speaker in that time period? This is one of the reasons the Bible is full of history—God works in real time with real people. (When I shared with my son that much of the Bible was history, an account of God working with his people, he was not very happy. At that time in his life, he did not like history.)

The Bible is not legend and myth. To understand the Psalms and the Prophets, the historical setting is vital. I need to know the historical context to understand the metaphors, idioms, and other aspects of the language. It is exciting to me to see new material being discovered that is helpful in this.

Look at the section in light of the whole book

Each book of the Bible was written as a unit. It has a theme, a purpose, and an occasion for being written. The identity of these will be found in the structure of the book. Some books have a clearer structure than others. I look for these as I study. Actually, many study Bibles give helpful information here. For example, Isaiah has been called a microcosm of the whole Bible. Isaiah has 66 chapters; the Bible has 66 books. The first 39 chapters of Isaiah deal primarily with history and judgment with some words of hope and comfort. God will continue to work through a remnant that stays faithful to Him. These are similar to the

Old Testament, which has 39 books, primarily history and judgment with words of hope and comfort. The last 27 chapters of Isaiah point to the future hope of restoration from captivity, to the Messiah, and to his kingdom. The New Testament has 27 books that tell of restoration, the Messiah, and his plans for the present and the future. I place the portion being studied in the light of the part of the book in which it is found.

Look for timeless principles

Some commands and teachings, especially in the Old Testament, do not seem to fit our day. One needs to find the principle behind the command, so we can apply it to our lives today. A principle is universal in nature, not dependent on time or culture. An understanding of the above-mentioned practices helps in this particular process. For example, it says in Leviticus 11:7, do not eat pork. The issue is not necessarily eating pork. There are at least two principles. One is health-related. The other is the separation of God's people to Himself. Not eating pork was one way to keep the Israelites from becoming one with the culture around them. In our culture, pork is no longer a heath risk. In our day, holiness or separation to God is more a matter of the heart.

For the kingdom of God is not a matter of eating and drinking, but of righteousness, peace and joy in the Holy Spirit. (Romans 14:17)[1]

---

[1] Scripture references are from the New International Version of the Bible.

Apply to practical daily living

I look for ways that the scripture I am reading can transform or influence various aspects of my total being. What does God want to do in my spirit? What does God want me to choose? What does God want me to think or to change in my perspective? What does God want me to do with my emotions? These questions are directed to the different elements of human personality. What does God want me to do? What does God want to do in my social context? All of these questions may not apply to the particular scripture I may be studying, but over a period of time, all these questions help me apply the teaching to my total being to:

1. Shape my thoughts
2. Guide every dimension of my life
3. Build relationships
4. Minister to others and
5. Reach out to others

The Bible has to first speak to my own condition and to me before I can share it with others. The above principles have been most helpful in my own growth and in my ministry to others.

Application to a Specific Text

The book of the Bible I will apply these principles to is Isaiah. The man Isaiah is one of the Major Prophets in the Old Testament. A prophet has at least two major functions: one is to carry the message God gave them to correct or encourage God's people and other nations, and the other is to tell of future events.

To understand the message of a prophet, historical context is vital. Isaiah does this in the first verse:

The vision concerning Judah and Jerusalem that Isaiah son of Amoz saw during the reigns of Uzziah, Jotham, Ahaz and Hezekiah. (Isaiah 1:1)

The reader can go to the historical section of scripture that tells the story of theses kings in Chapters 15-20 of 2 Kings and Chapters 26-32 of 2 Chronicles. They reveal that Isaiah ministered during the good reigns of Uzziah, Jotham, and Hezekiah. However, "Ahaz ... did not do what was right in the eyes of the Lord his God" (2 Kings 16:2). Isaiah received his call at the death of Uzziah: Go and give God's message. His response is well known: "Here I am, send me" (Isaiah 6:8). He was to preach to a people who would not listen and were facing judgment. Yet a remnant would remain.

The northern Kingdom of Israel had already fallen to Assyria. The Israelites had been exiled to foreign lands to live. Defeated peoples from other lands were brought into Israel. The same fate awaited the southern Kingdom of Judah and other surrounding nations. Assyria and later Babylon were a constant threat to Judah. Eventually, Babylon would invade and defeat Judah under the leadership of Nebuchadnezzar. Isaiah's message from God was an invitation from God to listen to reason.

"Come now, let us reason together," says the Lord
"Though your sins are like scarlet, they shall be as white as snow: though they are red as crimson, they shall be like wool. If you are willing and obedient, you will eat the best from the land; but if you resist and rebel, you will be

*devoured by the sword." For the mouth of the Lord has
spoken. (Isaiah 1:18-20)*

The first thirty-nine chapters of this book were probably
written around 700 BC, while the last twenty-seven
chapters were probably written near the end of his life
around 681 B.C. This was almost a century before
Nebuchadnezzar captured Jerusalem. Because of the
differences between these two sections, some think that
two different people had to write the book of Isaiah. There
are no solid reasons for this. One man, who had a long life
of service, wrote in two different periods of his life under
different circumstances. One section speaks of the
judgment to come; the other of the comfort and hope we
have in the midst of darkness.

In the midst of Judah's impending judgment and in the
face of his own death, Isaiah wrote these powerful words:

Comfort, comfort my people, says your God. (Isaiah 40:1)

One of the roles of those with pastoral gifts in our
meetings, is to bring comfort to those who are suffering
and afraid. This comfort is often based on the teaching in
the remainder of Isaiah.

In Chapters 40-48, Isaiah prophesies that God's people
will be delivered from captivity and Babylon judged; God
is revealed as the one true God; Isaiah presents the case
that God is greater than any idol or false representation of
God; and the Jews have not worshipped idols since. He
gives us a picture of what God is like. In Chapters 49-59,
he tells us about the future redeemer—the messiah, the
suffering servant. This section, especially Chapter 53,
contains some of the most powerfully descriptive verses

about Jesus. This is prophecy about the first coming of Christ. Chapters 60-66 prophesy about the future kingdom. They portray, in some of the most wonderful descriptions, what life is like where God rules. These three sections are full of truth and promises that comfort. They empower God's people.

The paragraph I want to center on is found in Chapter 40. As you will notice, I will apply it to others and to myself—that is what people with the pastoral gift do. I process it in my own life; and then I seek to help others see themselves in the text. This section's teaching will point to the theme of comfort and God's deliverance. In the midst of suffering, it is easy to doubt God's love and concern. It was true for the remnant in captivity, longing for God's deliverance and justice; it has been true for Christians over the centuries; it is true for us today. They wondered if God cared. They wondered if they had the power and strength to endure and overcome.

Questioning is often the beginning of understanding. The people of Judah were complaining and questioning God. Some gracious truth stands out. God does not condemn this questioning. God gives His people room to express doubt and pain. The answers to the questions in the text give us room to express our situation and feelings. Even though in our heart of hearts we know God already knows, we are given permission to share our perceptions with him and to cry out our doubt.

Isaiah 40:27-31

27 *Why do you say, O Jacob,*
and complain, O Israel,
"My way is hidden from the LORD;
my cause is disregarded by my God"?
28 *Do you not know? Have you not heard?*
The LORD is the everlasting God,
the Creator of the ends of the earth.
He will not grow tired or weary,
and his understanding no one can fathom.
29 *He gives strength to the weary*
and increases the power of the weak.
30 *Even youths grow tired and weary,*
and young men stumble and fall;
31 *but those who hope in the LORD will*
renew their strength.
They will soar on wings like eagles;
they will run and not grow weary,
they will walk and not be faint.

As I said above, my first bout with depression came after I, in obedience to God, quit teaching to study the Bible. My wife became ill, my son developed asthma, and I had to drop out of school for a time because of illness. I could not work. There were bills to pay. I had dark and foreboding thoughts. Is this what happens to people who just want to do God's will? Day after day, I questioned God's goodness and love. Had He forgotten my family and me?

God responds in verse 28 with two questions. "Do you not know? Have you not heard?" God uses Isaiah to challenge me, to challenge us. Our answer probably would be "yes"—a hesitant yes, a tentative yes. In our heads, we may be familiar with what is to come, but we have not experienced it deeply in our soul. There is a gentleness in God's approach to us in suffering and seeking to understand. He does not cram truth down our throats. He feeds us piece by piece what we can handle.

Next, Isaiah begins to share truth about God to fill in missing parts of our knowledge. Or, he shares to remind us of truth we already know but have not fully grasped. He starts with God: "The Lord is the everlasting God, the creator of the ends of the earth." God is not locked in time—but sees the whole picture. We can understand some of the past; we experience the present; but it is difficult for us to see the future. Where is all this going to lead? God is Lord; He knows what He is doing. Jesus is the master teacher; He knows what lessons we need now to prepare us for the future. God is creator; He knows us well—our limitations, our struggles, our needs, our challenges. Our response to such knowledge is faith and trust.

In the midst of my depression one verse from Job became a source of comfort and hope: "Though He slay me, yet will I trust Him" (Job 13:15).

God is omnipotent. Jehovah is all-powerful. "He will not grow tired or weary." We grow weary and exhausted. Life and ministry often overwhelm me. God is never overwhelmed. God is omniscient and all knowing. "And his understanding no one can fathom." God knows all our deepest needs. By faith and trust, we recognize the wisdom of God in the written word and in dealing with our lives. As we learn to trust Christ, we find that Jesus is the power of God and the wisdom of God (see 1 Corinthians 1:24).

In the midst of my depression, I heard the call of God to pastor. That period in my life prepared me to pastor. I could not have ministered to others or shared the knowledge of God without experiencing His goodness, wisdom, and power in my time of need.

God empowers his people. "He gives strength to the weary and increases the power of the weak. Even youths grow tired and weary, and young men stumble and fall; but those who hope in the Lord will renew their strength." Jesus invites the weary to come to him. "Come to me, all you who are weary and burdened, and I will give you rest" (Matthew 11:28). Paul tells that when we are weak, Christ is strong. He quotes a word he hears from the Lord. "My grace is sufficient for you, for my power is made perfect in weakness" (2 Corinthians 12:9).

How is this strength renewed in our lives? "Those who hope in the Lord will renew their strength." The word for "hope" in the Hebrew is not easily translated into English. It is translated at least two other ways: as "wait" in the New American Standard Version of the Bible and "trust" in the Jewish Publication Society Hebrew-English *Tanakh*. I used to believe that waiting meant one sat and waited passively until God put something in me. There is a place for that, but waiting in scripture is also actively seeking and trusting in God to act. It is meditating on His Word. It involves seeking counsel from others. It is looking for openings God may have from others. It involves asking the Holy Spirit to guide and illuminate.

In my waiting, I asked God to show me if there was anything in my life that was not in line with his Word. Over and over again, I quoted Job 13:15 and other promises in the Bible. During my seeking and waiting, God brought along a fellow student who calmly and gently ministered to me. The Holy Spirit began to take scripture and teaching and burn it into my heart. New hope and strength came. I could not be the pastor I am without the humility and gratitude these experiences brought into my life.

This section closes with three promises to those who trust in and wait on the Lord: "They will soar on wings like eagles." This lesson presents a picture from nature of beauty and perspective. We do not have many eagles where I live, but we do have red-tailed hawks. They spread out their wings on the air and drafts allow them to glide and soar. No longer grounded, they see a whole new perspective below. We can also begin to see God's perspective and understanding of the difficult times in life. "They will run and not grow weary." Weariness will come, but we will seek God for renewal of strength to go on. "They will walk and not be faint."

As one who ran cross-country in college, this speaks to me. One practice stands out in my mind. The coach had us run our usual two to three mile warm up and a few wind sprints. Then we moved to the next part of the practice: run one mile in five and one-half minutes, rest sixty seconds, then do another. We ended up running twenty miles, one at a time. By the end of practice, we were weary, but the next day, we were running again. Walking is more my speed now. I walk more than I run. The pace may be slower, but it is still one step at a time. In the difficult times, we will persevere, one step at a time.

God is with us; Jehovah knows us and where we are. In the midst of life's most difficult times, we will find that God knows what He is doing. God is trustworthy and powerful—His comfort keeps us and encourages us.

Developing Your Own Discipline in Studying the Bible

These are hints that have helped me consistently stay in the Bible.

Set a time and place that works best for you

I usually like the morning best. My wife often likes late at night best. You have to find a time that works for you. Consistency is more important than the time of day.

Set a plan

In getting started, I usually encourage a student to start with one book and become very familiar with it. There are certain books that we relate to more than others. A friend of mine calls these "core books." It is difficult to master every book in the Bible. I seek to stay familiar with every book, but there are core books from which I can teach on the spur of the moment. Some of my core books are John, Romans, Ephesians, Philippians, and Colossians. I have various Psalms that are core. As you read through the Bible, look for the books that you relate to quickly. As I said before, I read the Bible through two to three times a year to stay familiar with every book.

Keep a pen handy

I use a pen as a bookmark in my reading and study of the Bible. I underline, write questions in the margin, and write the date. I often use what I discover in journaling—I write in my journal the thoughts or new understandings that come. I process the emotions that come from reading the text or, rather, I use the text to process emotions I am having.

Discern between "milk" and "meat"

These are two metaphors used to describe the Bible. The milk verses are those that need no or little explanation. I have several of these from when I started reading the Bible. Isaiah 41:10 ("So do not fear, for I am with you: do not be dismayed, for I am our God. I will strengthen you and help you; I will uphold you with my righteous right hand") is an example of such a verse. Most I have memorized. The meat verses are those that are difficult to understand. I still have some of those I am chewing on. I encourage people not give up when they choke on the meat. Isaiah 63:1-6 takes a little more digging and chewing to understand. Keep reading. I find that some verses take years to understand. Keep chewing on the difficult verses.

Keep at it

I think I finally have this discipline down. There are frequent starts and stops—that is part of the process of developing a discipline that works for you. Don't give up just because you are not as consistent as you want to be. Get back on track as soon as you can.

Apply what you have read to every area of your life

I work daily on this. What does this scripture teach me about God? Is there something I need to do? Is there an attitude, thought, or emotion that this section refers to?

Share with others

I discover the more I share what I learn, the deeper the impression it makes on my own soul. Writing this chapter deepened my gratitude to God for all He has taught me in how to study His word to feed my soul and the souls of others. It has brought a deep sense of peace and a yearning to be faithful in handling His word (2 Timothy 2:15). This study in Isaiah has reminded me of the unity found in scripture and of the great heart God has for his people.

From my childhood, I have had the desire to know and serve God. This eventually led to a hunger to know and understand God's word and truth. I realized that one of God's primary ways to reveal Himself is through His word. Yet, I have been saddened by my own experience, in my life and my ministry, to see how few have taken the time to include the Bible in their search. Jesus is truth. His word is truth. I need both. I want others to know Jesus personally as their savior, Lord, and best friend. I trust that the principles and practices in this chapter will help others in their search for God and truth. I encourage you to start now and take the first steps to becoming immersed in the Bible.

My prayers are with you.

Bibliography

Adler, Mortimer J. & Charles van Doren. *How to Read a Book*. New York: Simon and Schuster, 1972.

Clinton, J. Robert. *Having a Ministry That Lasts: Becoming a Bible Centered Leader*. Altadena, CA: Barnabas Publishers, 1997.

McQuilkin, J. Robertson. *Understanding and Applying the Bible*. Chicago: Moody Press, 1983.

Stephen W. Angell is the Geraldine C. Leatherock Professor of Quaker Studies at the Earlham School of Religion. He is currently a member of (and Clerk of) Oxford Monthly Meeting in Oxford, Ohio, part of Ohio Valley Yearly Meeting. His past Quaker leadership positions include being Clerk of Southeastern Yearly Meeting (1999-2001). He is the author of articles on William Penn's theology, Early Quaker views of the book of Colossians, Rufus Jones' view of missions, and the interaction of Quaker missionaries with Buddhists in China and Japan, among others. He is also the author of *Bishop Henry McNeal Turner and African-American Religion in the South* and co-edited (with Anthony Pinn) *Social Protest Thought in the African Methodist Episcopal Church, 1862-1939*. He lives in Oxford with his wife, Sandra Ward-Angell, and two dogs and a cat.

THE LIGHT OF LIFE

Stephen W. Angell

How I Came to Love the Gospel of John

In the beginning was the Word, and the Word was with God, and the Word was God. (John 1:1)[1]

It is a grand beginning, one that brings to mind the very beginning of the First Testament:

In the beginning God created the heavens and the earth. (Geneis 1:1)

My beginnings were in a Quaker family. We lived in Pennsylvania until 1962 and then in New York State. I began to read the Bible not long after I received one as a Christmas gift from my grandfather Stephen LeRoy Angell, Sr., in 1961. I preferred the first verse of Genesis to the first verse of the Gospel of John, because I knew more intimately what it was that God had interacted with there. The heavens and the earth I knew. I gazed up into one, and I rested on the other. That both should have been fashioned for my friends and me by a loving creator seemed utterly natural. But the Word: just what exactly was the Word? And why should it be of concern to me? It

---

[1] Except as otherwise noted, all scripture quotations are from the Gospel of John in the New Revised Standard Version.

seemed so distant and so abstract, unlike the witty, earthy, and ethically demanding Jesus of the Synoptic Gospels.

My reaction was not unusual for the northeastern Quaker meetings of which I was a part. I do not remember the Gospel of John being brought into meeting life, either during meeting for worship or during First Day School. The Sermon on the Mount and stories of Noah, Abraham, Jacob, Samson, Gideon, David, and Solomon were prominently featured in First Day School—but not John's Gospel. This omission was not justified, at least in my presence, but it may have had something to do with the very straightforward way in which the author of the Gospel identifies Jesus as an incarnation of God. The meetings that I attended would have leaned in the direction of a Unitarian conception of God, so John's take on the subject would have been frowned upon.

It was only when I was able to put the Fourth Gospel in the context of my Quaker beliefs that it began to make any sense to me. In 1975, I purchased a copy of the Nickalls edition of George Fox's *Journal.* While I did not then read all the way through the *Journal,* I read deeply enough into it that I sensed the reality to which Fox testified. The loving God who made heavens and earth was also the inward Teacher who had come to teach his people himself. Having grown up in a Quaker meeting, most of what Fox had written seemed quite familiar to me, but it also had a depth and searching power that brought me to a deeper place in contemplating the spiritual and material worlds around me.

In 1979, a friend lent me a New Testament in a fresh translation, the New English Bible (NEB). This book I read from cover to cover. This time it was the Gospel of John that most reached my heart. Perhaps my new appreciation of it was that I was reading it in part with Fox's eyes. "The real light which enlightens every man was even then coming into the world"(1:9, NEB). I may have read this verse before, but this was the first time that I had so powerfully connected it with the inner light, or the Inward Teacher. "Such are the worshippers whom the Father wants. God is spirit, and those who worship him must worship in spirit and in truth" (4:25, NEB). Didn't this succinctly express the ideal of Quaker worship in which I partook at least once a week?

And I was electrified by John 15:12-16, which I could not recall having heard before:

This is my commandment: love one another, as I have loved you. There is no greater love than this, that a man should lay down his life for his friends. You are my friends, if you do what I command you. I call you servants no longer; a servant does not know what his master is about. I have called you friends, because I have disclosed to you everything that I heard from my Father. You did not choose me: I chose you. I appointed you to go on and bear fruit, fruit that shall last. (NEB)

So that was where the name "Religious Society of Friends" had come from! The designation of "Friends" seemed so much richer when grounded in a biblical text like this one. As a prison visitor, as well as someone who was thinking how the criminal justice system might profitably be reformed, it was helpful for me to see service and friendship linked in this fashion. Not only was I serving society (both the Religious Society of Friends and the broader society) by working on behalf of prisoners, but I was being friends with Jesus, and lots of other people. The Gospel of John was helping me to make sense of my world and to perceive another side of Jesus that I had previously missed.

The next First Day, I went to the Friends Meeting of Washington on Florida Avenue, and I sat on the facing bench, carrying the Bible my friend had loaned to me. In the silence, I was moved by the Spirit to stand and read these verses from the fifteenth chapter of John. I shared a few comments on what these verses meant to me. When I sat down, the silence seemed to deepen, and there were several heartfelt sharings out of the silence on the theme that I had raised. I remember neither my words, nor the words of those who spoke afterwards, but I left the meetinghouse feeling that the Spirit had favored us with a gathered meeting that day, and that my faithfulness to the Spirit's promptings had something to do with it.

In 1980, the Spirit led me to undertake theological studies at the Earlham School of Religion. The next eight years gave me many opportunities to read and to ponder John's Gospel, as I gained a Master of Arts degree in Quaker Studies from E.S.R. and later a Ph.D. degree in the History of Christianity at Vanderbilt University. Then I began teaching, with fulfilling appointments at Florida A&M University in Tallahassee (1990-2001) and at the Earlham School of Religion (2001-present). I grew in my appreciation of this gospel, as I meditated on its extensive influences on the early Quaker theologians I had come to love—George Fox, William Penn, and Robert Barclay.

Two Ways of Reading John's Gospel

My encounter with John's Gospel in Washington, D.C., had opened an exciting new window for me on John's Gospel and even on Christianity as a whole. My earliest exposures to this gospel had left me alienated from it, wondering if there was any way that I could call myself Christian. On the other hand, reading in company with George Fox,[2] resulted in ministry in meeting that seemed edifying and may have contributed to a gathered meeting, and helped me build a sense of vocation as a Christian minister, so much so that I shortly decided to enroll in a Quaker seminary. How can we make sense of these different interpretations of the same text?

In fact, divergent readings of this gospel are deeply rooted in hundreds of years of Christian history. I submit that it can help us all understand our Quakerism better if we can understand these two readings of the Gospel of John in greater depth. It would help this discussion if we could focus a little more sharply within the Gospel of John. I propose to focus my discussion on the first eighteen verses of John's Gospel—the part that is usually referred to as the Prologue.

What we find in these verses is a series of propositions about a person, Jesus, also known as the Christ, who is not named until the next-to-last verse:

----

[2] My phraseology here (reading in the company of, or as a friend of, George Fox) is influenced by Michael Birkel, *Engaging Scripture: Reading the Bible with Early Friends.*

John 1:1-18

¹ *In the beginning was the Word, and the Word was with God, and the Word was God.* ² *He was in the beginning with God.* ³ *All things came into being through him, and without him not one thing came into being. What has come into being* ⁴ *in him was life, and the life was the light of all people.* ⁵ *The light shines in the darkness, and the darkness did not overcome it.*

⁶ *There was a man sent from God, whose name was John.* ⁷ *He came as a witness to testify to the light, so that all might believe through him.* ⁸ *He himself was not the light, but he came to testify to the light.* ⁹ *The true light, which enlightens everyone, was coming into the world.*

¹⁰ *He was in the world, and the world came into being through him; yet the world did not know him.* ¹¹ *He came to what was his own, and his own people did not accept him.* ¹² *But to all who received him, who believed in his name, he gave power to become children of God,* ¹³ *who were born, not of blood or of the will of the flesh or of the will of man, but of God.*

¹⁴ *And the Word became flesh and lived among us, and we have seen his glory, the glory as of a father's only son, full of grace and truth.* ¹⁵ *(John testified to him and cried out, "This was he of whom I said, 'He who comes after me ranks ahead of me because he was before me.'")* ¹⁶ *From his fullness we have all received, grace upon grace.* ¹⁷ *The law indeed was given through Moses; grace and truth came through Jesus Christ.* ¹⁸ *No one has ever seen God. It is God the only Son, who is close to the Father's heart, who has made him known.*

Verses 1-3: The author asserts that Christ, as the Word which was with God and also was God, pre-existed the creation of the world and was intimately involved in the act of creation.

Verse 4: True life came into being through him, and that "life was the light of all people."

Verses 6-9: A man named John was a witness to this light, but not the light itself. Christ, however, is the true light which enlightens everyone.

Verse 5, 10, & 11: The light met opposition, in the form of darkness or ignorance or rejection by the people to whom he would belong in human form, but these opposing forces were not granted the ultimate victory.

Verse 5, 12, & 13:The darkness did not put out the light, and all who believed in Christ were empowered "to become children of God," born of God.

Verse 14: The Word, initially disembodied, "became flesh and lived among us." This incarnated Word Christ showed forth the glory of "God the father's only son, full of grace and truth."

Verse 18: Christ is close to the Father's heart, and it is this Christ who has made God the father known to the world.

By any account, this is an extraordinary assessment of Christ. No other written gospel known to us begins in a remotely similar fashion. Mark's gospel begins with an account of Jesus' baptism. Luke's and Matthew's gospels begin with stories of a miraculous conception, accompanied by genealogies which trace Jesus' ancestry back to Abraham (in Matthew's telling) or to Adam (in Luke's rendition). John's gospel trumps all of these by placing Christ's origins even prior to the creation. So he makes the greatest claims of all.

Many Christians would accept all of the propositions made about Christ in John's prologue as true. Early Quakers certainly would have accepted and believed in all of these propositions. One step, however, that is crucial in deciding how to interpret John's prologue, and indeed the whole rest of John's gospel, is to ask: Which of these propositions are most important? Which constitutes the culminating part of John's argument? Which provides the organizing principle around which we can arrange all of the rest of these propositions?

It is on this point that early Quakers (and many modern-day Quakers) differed from virtually all of their Christian contemporaries. Quakers saw the pivotal and culminating insight of the Prologue in the affirmation of verse 9 that Christ is the true light who enlightens every one, whereas most Christians have identified the pivot with verse 14 announcing the Word made flesh, that is, the entrance of the Christ Spirit into history in the specific incarnated form of Jesus of Nazareth. The verse 9 view places the greatest emphasis on the universal and spiritualized saving nature and availability of an immanent Christ, both in the present moment and throughout the whole of human history, and demands that people realize the maximum redemptive possibilities of every living moment. The verse 14 view, however, emphasizes the pivotal nature of a particular historical moment, and demands that Christians come to an understanding of how the life, death, and resurrection of a human being who lived two thousand years ago has been productive of a salvation that, while available to all, must be explicitly accepted or claimed.

R. Alan Culpepper is a modern Johannine scholar who has given fine expression to the central importance in John's Gospel of what I call "verse 9 spirituality." Culpepper calls attention to the great importance of symbolism in the Gospel of John, part of an extensive system of implicit communication, of "subsurface signals" conveyed, as it were, by "various nods, winks, and gestures." Of these implicit themes in the gospel, Culpepper identifies "light" as one of the three most important:

> The three core symbols of the gospel are light, water, and bread. Each of these points to Jesus' revelatory role and carries a heavy thematic load. To these are related several coordinate symbols, metaphors, and concepts in different passages: darkness, life, wine, flesh. Subordinate symbols can be gathered around each. For example, among the subordinate symbols for light are lamps, fires, torches, lanterns, day (and night), morning, seeing, and healing the blind.[3]

The power of this symbol begins with the prologue and carries through the entire gospel. For example, in Chapter 9 of the gospel, Jesus gives sight to a blind man, but that blind man symbolizes all of us: "In Johannine thought all are born blind, and sight is always given." By the end of the gospel, the symbol of light has "expanded to the point of explosion so that the mere suggestions of its presence

---

[3] Culpepper, *Anatomy of the Fourth Gospel*, 189.

evoke the heavy thematic and theological load it acquired in its earlier, more explicit development."

This kind of exploration of the symbolism of light in John's gospel is unusual in the sweep of Christian history. Culpepper may refer to "flesh" as a "coordinate symbol," but generally, more emphasis has been given to what I call the verse 14 view, focusing on the Word made flesh. Here is an exploration from the Swiss Reformer John Calvin of the verse 14 view. In a section entitled "The sole purpose of Christ's incarnation was our redemption," Calvin observes:

> All Scripture proclaims that to become our Redeemer he was clothed with flesh . . . We well know why Christ was promised from the beginning: to restore the fallen world and to succor lost men. . . . When he himself appeared, he declared that the reason for his advent was to gather us from death unto life. The apostles testified to the same thing concerning him. So John, before he teaches that "the Word was made flesh," [John1:14] tells of man's rebellion. [John 1:9-11][4]

For Calvin, Verse 9 was a subsidiary verse, one that signified spiritual death and showed why the redemption was necessary, whereas verse 14 was the crux of the matter, the essence of the entire meaning or import of scripture. Christ's outward atonement, his willingness to bear the punishment for our sins by his death on the cross at Calvary, is the whole basis of our Christian hope.

---

[4] Calvin, *Institutes*, 2.12.4.

However, Calvin's opposition, Radical Reformers such as Menno Simons, (founder of the Mennonites) disputed with him on precisely this point. For Menno Simons, Christ's spiritual nature was paramount. He believed that Christ had celestial flesh, or in other words, that Jesus was a "heavenly man." According to Menno, the infant Jesus had been carried in Mary's womb, but Jesus' kinship with God entailed a perfection that must not be tainted by his having anything in common with her flesh. In other words, Jesus had about as much to do with Mary as flowing water does with a pipe. To counter Simons, Calvin felt that he had to emphasize a strongly incarnational view of Christian doctrine based on verse 14. Richard Bailey has shown that George Fox's Christology was not very different from Menno's, so it is not far-fetched to see Calvin as anticipating and answering future arguments from theologians such as Fox.

While early Quaker theologians did not follow Menno Simons in emphasizing the spiritual side of Christ to such an extent as to deny his human side, they definitely subordinated the outward Christ to the spiritual Word that has existed from before the creation of the world. James Nayler clearly expresses the Quakers' earliest view of verse 14:

Concerning Jesus Christ, [we believe] that he is the eternal word of God, "by whom all things were made," and are upheld . . . which "word became flesh, and dwelt amongst" the saints; who is "the same yesterday, to-day, and for ever;" who did and doth dwell in the saints; who suffered, and rose again, and ascended into heaven, and is set at the right hand of God, to whom "all power is given in heaven and in earth;" who fills all places, is the light of the world, but known to none but to those that receive and follow him, and those he leads up to God, out of all the ways, works, and worships of the world, by his pure light in them, whereby he reveals "the man of sin;" and by his power casts him out, and so prepares the bodies of the saints a fit temple for the pure God to dwell in.[5]

While Nayler acknowledges the incarnation, he sees Christ's significance in his spiritual essence, first as the eternal Word of God involved in the creation, but mostly in Christ's existence as a "pure light" within the saints.

Thus, while Fox and Nayler clearly took notice of verse 14, their rather insistent and incessant emphasis was on verse 9. This emphasis can be found throughout the early pages of George Fox's *Journal*. Here is one sampling:

Christ it was who had enlightened me, that gave me his light to believe in, and gave me hope, which is himself, revealed himself in me, and gave me his spirit, and gave me his grace, which I found sufficient in the deeps and in weakness. . . . As the Light appeared, all appeared that is out of the Light, darkness, death, temptations, the unrighteous, the ungodly; all was manifest and seen in the Light. . . John, who was the greatest prophet that was born of

---

[5] James Naylor [sic], *Collection of Sundry Books*, 64 (Digital Quaker Collection, hereafter abbreviated DQC).

a woman, did bear witness to the light, which Christ the great heavenly prophet hath enlightened every man that cometh into the world withal, that they might believe in it, and become the children of the light, and so have the light of life.[6]

For every mention of verse 14 in early Quaker writings, there are one hundred mentions or allusions to verse 9, so much so that by the time Robert Barclay was writing his *Apology for the True Christian Divinity* in the 1670s he could refer to verse 9 as the "Quakers' text."

While many interpreters of this gospel have suggested that the statement that "I am the light of the world" found in John 8:12 should be understood as applying to the outward Jesus, early Quakers were more inclined to see this statement as applying to the inward Christ. George Fox counseled his readers to "know this wisdom, that excels folly and darkness, and comprehends it, which gives to see the salvation Christ Jesus, the light of the world, that doth enlighten every man that cometh into the world."[7] Of John 8:12, Elizabeth Bathurst wrote, "Praised be the Lord, there is a remnant who have experienced it, and can say with the Apostle, this Thing is true in them, viz. The Darkness is past and the true Light now shineth."[8] In other words, the most important work of the "light of the world" is internal, in each person's heart and mind.

---

[6] Fox, *Journal*, 12-16.

[7] George Fox, *Testimony of the True Light of the World*, 19 (DQC).

[8] Elizabeth Bathurst, *Truth Vindicated*, 100 (DQC).

This line of analysis opens the question as to whether it is possible to heal divisions between advocates of verse 9 spirituality and verse 14 spirituality. I believe that there is such a possibility. My church historical readings would suggest that much of these divisions arose five hundred years ago during the Reformation, and as I read theologians from the first four Christian centuries, I don't see nearly as much bifurcation in interpretations between these various aspects of John's prologue. For example, Augustine of Hippo was able to blend together verse 9 and verse 14 perspectives quite harmoniously. In *Faith and the Creed*, Augustine wrote:

> The Word became flesh and dwelt among us" (John 1:14). The Wisdom who was begotten of God deigned to be created among men. . . . According to his nature as first-born, he has deigned to call brethren all who, after him and by means of his headship, are born again into the grace of God by adoption as sons. . . . Being Son by nature he was born uniquely of the substance of the Father, being what the Father is, God of God, Light of Light. We are not light by nature, but we are illumined by that light, according as we are able to shine in wisdom. "He was the true light that lighteth every man coming into this world" (John 1:9).[9]

What would it look like for twenty-first-century Quakers to follow Augustine's lead on this issue and lend their efforts to a convergence of verse 9 and verse 14

---

[9] Augustine, *Faith and the Creed*, 356-357.

spirituality? One way we might address such a question is to ask what verse 9 and verse 14 have in common. Both are life giving in the most profound sense, and both (in somewhat different ways, to be sure) help illuminate that life-giving reality we find in the Jesus who we call the Christ. Both are grounded deeply in the previous insights of John's prologue, particularly verse 4: "In him was life, and the life was the light of all people." The African-American theologian Howard Thurman, someone deeply appreciative of Quaker spirituality, utilized verse 4 in his attempt to explain how Jesus ought to be regarded, given the irony of a sometimes oppressive institutional Christianity that happened to arise despite Jesus' own liberating, justice-oriented personal witness:

> The basic fact is that Christianity as it was born in the mind of this Jewish teacher and thinker appears as a technique of survival for the oppressed. That it became, through the intervening years, a religion of the powerful and the dominant, used sometimes as an instrument of oppression, must not tempt us into believing that it was thus in the mind and life of Jesus. "In him was life; and the life was the light of men." Wherever his spirit appears, the oppressed gather fresh courage; for he announced that fear, hypocrisy, and hatred, the three hounds of hell that track the trail of the disinherited, need have no dominion over them.[10]

---

[10] Thurman, *Jesus and the Disinherited*, 29.

Whether we as Christians choose to highlight the aspect of Christ as Light or as Word made Flesh, we can, with Thurman, join in proclaiming and witnessing to the authentic life giving and liberating qualities of the gospel message we find in John's gospel and elsewhere.

Way, Truth, and Life

One of the most famous and controversial passages of the gospel of John occurs at the beginning of Jesus' farewell discourse in Chapter 14. Jesus informs the disciples that "you know the way to the place where I am going" (14:4). That provokes Thomas to observe, "Lord, we do not know where you are going. How can we know the way?" (14:5). Jesus memorably responds, "I am the way, the truth, and the life. No one comes to the Father except through me" (14:6).

For those who are caught up in verse 14 spirituality (whether proponents or opponents), this passage appears to carry with it an exclusivist message. Only a Christian, a known and committed follower of Jesus can obtain salvation, according to this line of interpretation. Of course, this leaves billions of Muslims, Hindus, Buddhists, and others outside of God's saving grace. If they are still alive, they have an opportunity to accept Christ and can still come to God the Father. But this opportunity must be grasped on this side of death.

Nothing could be further from the early Quaker interpretation of Chapter 14. John 14:6 was a favorite of early Quaker theologians, but it was consistently and insistently interpreted in an inclusive fashion. In one of the earliest Quaker tracts, *Newes coming up out of the north* (1653), Fox puts the matter this way, citing John 14:6:

> The letter saith, Christ is the light, and the light is but one, and it leads all one way, into one truth and unity, to be of one mind, one soul, one heart, to the Lord God of light, Father of Light...

So the light of Christ is what shows us the way, according to Fox. Many Puritan pastors disputed this point. William Penn, in the *Christian Quaker*, found John 14:6 to corroborate the following statement from the Greek philosopher Pythagoras, who lived five centuries prior to Jesus: "That it is Man's Duty to believe of the Divinity, . . . for the Divinity is such, that to it doth of Right belong the Dominion of all." This, then, is the Way and the Truth that Jesus spoke of, the deity witnessed by Pythagoras to which belongs the dominion over all. Again, Fox observed in 1671 that this Christ-like road to salvation must pass through the inward self in order to be genuine:

> The Way whereby a man must come, the Truth wherein he must be renewed, and the Life wherewith a man must be quickened, is Christ, the Son of the Living God, and he must know him as the Son of the Living God, and feel him revealed in him, and received by him, and so walk in him the Way, in him the Truth, in him the Life, if ever he come to the Father.[11]

---

[11] George Fox, *SomePprinciples of the Elect People of God*, 103 (DQC).

An outward knowledge of Christ is emphatically insufficient. In *Primitive Christianity Reviv'd*, William Penn noted that the essential lesson to be drawn from John 14:6 is that the Light of Christ can be viewed as "Truth in the Inward Parts." Isaac Penington used John 14:6 to establish that the scriptures can only be the secondary rule for the saints, because "the way is the rule, the truth is the rule, the life is the rule."[12] He equated these to "the writings of God's spirit, in the hearts of his people."

So the way, truth, and life pre-existed Jesus of Nazareth in the teachings of Pythagoras, and their most certain manifestation is not in the outward spirit but to the knowledge of God carried by all of God's people in their hearts. John 14:6 was a liberating text for Quakers when set firmly in the context of their Verse 9 Spirituality. A phrase commonly used by Friends throughout their history that "Way opens" (spoken when a spiritual barrier has been removed and something that seemed like an impossible or barely possible dream is now definitely an achievable reality) derives most directly from this verse.

So what Friends historically have most drawn from the Gospel of John is not knowledge of an outward Jesus, but certain characteristics of a Christ-like, mystical spirituality suitable to further meditative development. (One can properly term this Quaker reading of John as "mystical," if by that assertion one means that this text is a ready stimulus for a profound seeking for *and* finding of God within as well as without.) It is in this spirit that Rufus Jones has written that "Friends are essentially Johannine in

---

[12] Isaac Penington, *Works*, I, 462 (DQC).

their religious faith and outlook, [because] their great religious words are found in the Fourth Gospel. They are *light, truth, life, love, spirit, way.*"[13] And few Johannine texts were more significant for Friends than John 14:6, where they found a Way, a Truth, and a Life, not only in their own inward parts, but in the inward parts of anyone who was a sincere seeker after the Truth. But, in a practical sense, what does this internalized spirituality entail? To a Quaker, as to any Christian, the question that the evangelist in the Fourth Gospel places upon the lips of Pontius Pilate is quite relevant: What is truth? (18:38)

An Educator's Attempt to Walk in Truth

For Quakers, truth can never be mere belief, although belief in Christ is also a strong theme in the Gospel and Epistles of John. Rather, truth entails outward purpose and activity. God's children are to be found "walking in truth" (2 John 1:4). This is akin to saying that we should "walk in the light" (1 John 1:7; see also John 12:35-36), a formulation frequently used by Quakers even today. Even more succinctly, one must "do truth." As John 3:21 (KJV) states, "he that doeth truth cometh to the light."

Quaker books of Christian discipline are often subtitled, *Faith and Practice,* but faith can never be divorced from practice. Instead, faith ought to be seen as leading to practice. Stephen Grellet, a nineteenth century Quaker minister, lamented that among those interested in Quakerism, "there appears to be a spirit of religious

---

[13] Rufus M. Jones, *The Faith and Practice of the Quakers,* 15.

inquiry. Many wish to know what is Truth; but how few are willing to walk in it."

Parker Palmer's reflections on the spirituality of education have been helpful to me. Reflecting on these same Johannine verses, Parker states that Jesus' "call to truth is a call to community. . . . Truth involves a vulnerable, faithful, and risk-filled interpenetration of the knower and the known." The Christ made known to us by the Gospel of John helps to guide us into making our schools "living and evolving communit[ies] of creativity and compassion."[14]

I do not think that a Quaker appropriation of the Johannine Christian message leads to a unique, or even particularly distinctive, Quaker form of pedagogy. Quakers have no theories of teaching that are unique to ourselves. I do believe that the very basic, essential foundation for Quaker spirituality to be found in John's gospel provides a reliable grounding for a pedagogy that can at the same time be both solid and adventuresome.

I count myself fortunate to have taught at more than a half-dozen universities and seminaries, including, for the past five years, the first-established Quaker seminary, the Earlham School of Religion. But in the remaining space I have here, with these Johannine insights in mind, I would like to explore my experiences teaching religious studies for eleven years at Florida A&M University, a historically black university in Tallahassee. I taught every religious studies course that we had listed at some time during my

---

[14] Palmer, *To Know As We Are Known*, 14, 49.

tenure at FAMU, but the course that I taught most often was Black Religion in America.

It is quite pertinent to mention here that I am white, and that I had little exposure to anything that might be called a black church during my childhood. My passion for the subject, and my qualifications to teach it, were largely a product of my six years at Vanderbilt University during the 1980s. There, under the guidance of Professor Lewis V. Baldwin, I completed a dissertation on one of the towering leaders of nineteenth-century African-American religion, a bishop in the African Methodist Episcopal Church by the name of Henry McNeal Turner. The process of uncovering my passion for this subject, and then my joy in working on my dissertation, felt very much like a spiritual rebirth experience. Here was a calling, one worthy of my devotion and dedication. Here was truth that needed someone to witness to it. My passion for African-American religions did not displace my passion for Quakerism; rather, it felt complementary. I recognized that there was something about the passion for truth, love, and light in Quakerism (and John's Gospel) that was impelling me toward study of African-American religion, and that conversely, there was much in the truth, love, and light that I was discovering in African-American religions that I could bring back to my Quaker community.

For two years after receiving my Ph.D., I taught religion, including African-American religion, in historically white colleges in South Dakota and Ohio. Then, in 1990, I was called to join the faculty of Florida A&M University. I leaped at the chance to teach what I had come to know and love about African-American religion with a mostly African-American student body. But there was no escaping the fact that I was a white professor teaching black religion. How does one stay open to the Spirit of Truth under such circumstances? How does one attend to the Light of Christ in everybody in the classroom, and model the friendship of which Jesus had spoken so eloquently in John 15? Was it even appropriate for me to be teaching the subject that had become my great love and had been the focus of my doctoral studies?

To be perfectly honest, there were a number of persons within the Florida A&M University community who thought it inappropriate for me to be teaching that subject. There was enough controversy on the issue that the Philosophy and Religion department held a well-attended forum, and the student newspaper, the *Famuan*, editorialized on the subject. I welcomed the honest discussion on the issue, and of course was pleased when the *Famuan* editorial backed my teaching of the course. But all of this, for me at least, was a sideshow to the main event. How do I teach in this situation?

To a large degree, what sustained my teaching was the insights that I drew from the Gospel of John and appropriations of it such as Parker Palmer's. My classroom had to be a living and evolving community of creativity and compassion. While I intended my class to have academic rigor, I also tried to model a spirit of listening and openness. I wanted my students to learn from me, but I also wanted to learn from them. My first assignment in the class was always for them to write a religious autobiography, in which, if they chose, they could address the question of what is black about black religion? As you can imagine, I got an amazingly large variety of answers to that question. My students' inner light and devotion to truth shown clearly through their delightfully varied witness.

Always, there was space for questions and feedback. One day, when I had filled the board with names of black women who were religious leaders, I had a student who walked into class that day and said, "I know someone whose name belongs on that board." So I learned that day about Biddy Moore, the woman who was the chief founder of the First A.M.E. Church of Los Angeles.

Occasionally the discussion in the classroom grew heated, but I still welcomed and invited it and worked at remaining non-defensive (not always succeeding!) But it helped to reflect that the Truth for which we all are striving was much bigger than anyone of us, including the instructor in the class. I returned again and again to these words of Jesus, from John 8:31-32: "If you continue in my word, you are truly my disciples; and you will know the truth, and the truth will make you free." Knowing the truth here is contingent upon obedience to Christ. For me, that meant that Love and Light, as well as Truth, had to be guiding forces in my classroom. I could not simply master the truth; I had to be open to the assurance that truth would master me as well.

When not at Quaker Meeting, I would often enjoy visiting one of the many African American churches in the Tallahassee community. I found that the song, prayer, even the shouting, could nurture that same divine center within me that Quaker silence does. Or, in the language of the Gospel of John, I came to know experimentally that "in my Father's house there are many dwelling places" (14:2). Not all are explicitly Christian. Sometimes a Muslim student would ask me why my teaching focused so much on black Christianity. I had various answers for that question, including my conviction on the centrality of Christianity in the African-American religious experience and my own love for African-American Christianity. But my Muslim students helped to keep me honest. And I came to love and respect African-American Islam, in its various forms, as well. I stayed in Tallahassee long enough, that when I visited African-American churches, sometimes a former student would be preaching, often after going on to complete a Master of Divinity degree. Just like the Quaker meetinghouse, the Light and Love and Truth that I found in the religious studies classroom often dissolved the walls of the room and flowed out into the world—and then returned to the classroom.

Conclusion

While the foregoing is an honest statement of the importance of the Fourth Gospel in the life of one Quaker educator, I have not attempted to provide a full summary of the Gospel itself. I have concerned myself little with the first-century context of John's Gospel, with the sharp controversies between Jews and Christians that helped to give it its final shape, or with scholarly judgments about the Johannine community that helped to give this gospel its finely textured substance, probably over more than one generation. It is true that the historical context in which a biblical book was written is very important and that one should find out about it in order to gain a deeper understanding of it. I encourage my readers not only to read the Gospel of John again for themselves, but also to locate and to read more resources that will deepen their appreciation of it.

What I have argued in this essay is the importance of certain spiritual, inward, and mystical realities in the Gospel of John, especially Light, Life, and Truth. As I have grown more familiar with the gospel, I found the gospel's development of these spiritual realities helpful in my growth as a teacher and as a person. Also, I claim to read this gospel in a particular interpretive tradition. I read it as a friend of George Fox and other Quakers over a three-and-a-half century time span. This interpretive tradition finds what Culpepper has called the symbolism of the gospel to be of particular importance. Reading in this tradition, I often value the gospel's symbolic insights more than some aspects of the gospel's plot. In fact, I find reflection on these spiritual, symbolic realities to be an indispensable part of my spiritual growth and my participation in worship. It is on this basis that I can so heartily commend this gospel to others. I hope that I have helped this gospel to speak to you.

Bibliography

Anderson, Paul N. *Navigating the Living Waters of the Gospel of John: On Wading with Children and Swimming with Elephants.* Pendle Hill Pamphlet, 352. Wallingford, PA: Pendle Hill Publications, 2000.

Augustine. *Augustine: Earlier Writings.* Ed. by J. H. S. Burleigh. The Library of Christian Classics. Philadelphia: Westminster Press, 1953.

Bailey, Richard. "Was Seventeenth-century Quaker Christology Homogenous?" In *The Creation of Quaker Theory.* Ed. by Pink Dandelion. Aldershot, Hants, England: Ashgate Publishing Limited, 2004, 61-82.

Birkel, Michael. *Engaging Scripture: Reading the Bible with Early Friends.* Richmond, IN: Friends United Press, 2005.

Calvin, John. *Institutes of the Christian Religion.* Ed. by John T. McNeill. The Library of Christian Classics. 2 Vols. Philadelphia: Westminster Press, 1960.

Culpepper, R. Alan. *Anatomy of the Fourth Gospel: A Study in Literary Design.* Philadelphia: Fortress Press, 1983.

Earlham School of Religion. Digital Quaker Collection. http://esr.earlham.edu/dqc/

Fuller, Georgia E. "Johannine Lessons in Community, Witness, and Power." In *The Bible, The Church & the Future of Friends.* Ed. by Chuck Fager. Wallingford, Pennsylvania: The Issues Program of Pendle Hill, 1996, 85-118.

Martyn, J. Louis. *History and Theology in the Fourth Gospel.* Nashville: Abingdon, 1979.

Palmer, Parker J. *To Know As We Are Known: A Spirituality of Education.* San Francisco: Harper and Row, 1986.

Simons, Menno. "Brief and Clear Confession." In *The Complete Writings of Menno Simons, c. 1496-1561.* Ed. by J. C. Wenger. Scottsdale, Pennsylvania: Herald Press, 1956, 419-455.

Thurman, Howard. *Jesus and the Disinherited.* Richmond, Indiana: Friends United Press, 1976.

Cathy Habschmidt is a life-long member of the Religious Society of Friends. She and her husband, Larry, live in Richmond, Indiana and have two young adult daughters. The Habschmidts are members of Clear Creek Monthly Meeting in Ohio Valley Yearly Meeting. Cathy graduated from Olney Friends School (Barnesville, Ohio), Earlham College, and the Earlham School of Religion. She understands her current calling to be helping Friends communicate better with one another, despite our many differences, so that we can be more open to hearing the voice of God. Cathy is the Earlham College Controller and volunteers with Friends World Committee for Consultation, serving as Treasurer of the Section of the Americas, Clerk of the Campaign Steering Committee, and a member of the International Finance Committee.

LETTER AND SPIRIT: READING PAUL, LISTENING FOR GOD

Cathy Habschmidt

When I started reading the Bible, I was surprised to discover that fully one quarter of the New Testament was attributed to Paul. I had grown up in a liberal, unprogrammed Friends meeting, and my knowledge of the Bible was meager; I had no idea what a large role Paul played in scripture and indeed in the Christian tradition. My first impression of Paul, when I finally studied the Bible as an adult, was less than favorable. His treatment of women disturbed me, and his emphasis on the Cross rather than on the teachings of Jesus did not fit well with my theology at that time. In fact, I felt a growing sense of dismay and even anger that Paul's words had somehow been allowed to overshadow those of Jesus. The Gospel narratives had moved me from the start, but my appreciation for the letters of Paul was slower to evolve. I had much to learn.

Now when I read Paul, I remind myself that I'm reading documents fundamentally different from the Gospels of Matthew, Mark, Luke or John, or even the book of Acts. The four Gospels and Acts are written versions of stories that had been handed down orally for decades. Paul's letters, on the other hand, first existed in written form with the same content that I read in my New Testament today. I feel privileged to have direct access to the thoughts and feelings of one of the earliest Christians. The power and insight contained in Paul's letters can be a continuing source of inspiration for people like me nearly two thousand years after they were written.

Letters Written by Paul

Before we proceed much further, we need a word about authorship. In the first century, people often wrote in the name of another person This practice was common and even expected in certain situations. Scribes wrote in the name of public figures, sometimes by dictation and at other times simply on behalf of those figures. Students would append their teacher's name to their writings rather than their own name as a way to honor their mentors. Some people wrote in the name of an individual with whom they had no personal relationship, but whose work they admired. Simply because a letter says it was written by Paul does not mean that Paul was the actual author.

Most scholars today agree that some of the letters claiming to have been written by Paul were actually written long after Paul's death. When I talk about "reading Paul," I am referring only to those letters in the New Testament that are indisputably the work of Paul himself: Romans, 1 and 2 Corinthians, Galatians, Philippians, 1 Thessalonians, and Philemon. The other letters are certainly important and should not be discounted, but I believe they fall into a different category from the epistles undeniably written by Paul. Because both Paul as a particular person and the historical setting in which he wrote play a central role in how I read the letters of Paul, I am for the purposes of this discussion limiting my focus to just those seven letters.

Historical Context

The importance of considering the historical context in which Paul wrote cannot be overstated. Paul wrote each letter to a specific group of people or, in one case, to a particular individual. If he had known that a vastly wider audience would eventually read his epistles, he might have written them somewhat differently. By placing the letters in their appropriate contexts, we can begin to understand why Paul wrote as he did and, more importantly, what his words mean to us today.

Take 1 Thessalonians, for example. This letter to the church in the city of Thessalonica is widely accepted as the oldest writing in the entire New Testament. It was probably written only two decades after Jesus was crucified, or twenty to fifty years earlier than the Gospels. The Christian community was young, and Paul was just beginning his travels in the ministry.

The fundamental context for 1 Thessalonians is one common to most of Paul's letters: Paul is writing to the members of a church he had founded but from which he is now geographically separated. He desperately wants to maintain contact with his pupils and asks that his letter to the church community be read aloud to everyone (5:27). Current concerns for the church in Thessalonica include persecution by the authorities and, secondly, confusion about the return of Christ.

Paul's advice to the Thessalonians as they experience a period of persecution is priceless wisdom for all of us, in whatever difficult situations we may find ourselves:

> *See that none of you repays evil for evil, but always seek to do good to one another and to all. Rejoice always, pray without ceasing, give thanks in all circumstances; for this is the will of God in Christ Jesus for you. Do not quench the Spirit. Do not despise the words of prophets, but test everything; hold fast to what is good, abstain from every form of evil. (5:15-22)*

The timelessness of this guidance is transparent. These words harmonize beautifully with Friends' abhorrence of violence, even in self-defense, with our desire to help those less fortunate than ourselves, and indeed with our practice of testing leadings. Paul's words surely formed the basis for many of the Quaker testimonies.

The second part, however, of Paul's counsel to the Thessalonians may not make as much sense to us as we read it nearly two thousand years later. The imminent return of Christ was a major issue for early Christians. In the Gospel of Matthew, we learn of signs portending the return of Christ and are told that "this generation will not pass away until all these things have taken place" (24:34). Although the gospels were not written down until after Paul's death, he was no doubt aware of the many stories contained in them. Paul initially believed, and instructed his followers, that Jesus Christ would physically return to the earth within their lifetimes.

The obvious problem with this teaching, however, was the fact that members of the early Christian community did die. The remaining believers were left to worry whether their deceased loved ones would still be reunited with Christ when he finally arrived. This concern may sound silly to our modern ears, but it was of grave consequence for the Christians in Thessalonica. Paul felt compelled to offer them reassurance. He writes:

> *The dead in Christ will rise first. Then we who are alive, who are left, will be caught up in the clouds together with them to meet the Lord in the air; and so we will be with the Lord forever. Therefore encourage one another with these words. (4:16-18)*

Paul offers a slightly modified version of the end-times prediction in order to alleviate the fears of the Christians. He is motivated by his love for his followers but also, more importantly, by his understanding of God's love for humanity. When I read these particular words of Paul, I look past his specific vision of what might physically happen on earth and instead see the underlying message of God's enduring love and unwavering encouragement for us all. There is nothing, not even death, that can separate me from the love of God (Romans 8:38-39). As John Woolman said, "Love was the first motion." Love is the ultimate foundation of Paul's (and our) relationship with God and with one another.

Paul as a Real Person

One of my early challenges with reading Paul concerned the pedestal on which he appeared to stand. As a lifelong unprogrammed Friend, I am in the habit of seeing all members of my faith community as equals. I had trouble understanding how any person could be elevated to a position of power and authority almost as high, it seemed, as that of Jesus himself. Why were the words of Paul accepted as divinely inspired? How much weight should I place on his letters relative to the Gospels themselves? Was Paul a perfect Christian or was he as human (and fallible) as I am?

I discovered much later in my studies of the Bible that I was probably unduly influenced in my initial understanding of Paul by the author of Acts. The person who wrote the Acts of the Apostles was clearly a fan of Paul's, for he writes about Paul in a consistently favorable light. However, not once does the author of Acts mention any of Paul's letters, and indeed a few details in Acts are not quite consistent with parts of Paul's correspondence. I've concluded that the author of Acts knew more about the myth of Paul than about the true person, so I've been able to relax a bit and separate the story of Paul in Acts from the historical human being. In doing so, I've found myself much freer to see Paul as a flesh and blood person, someone from whom I can learn a great deal but also someone in whom I can see my own human foibles.

We get a vivid glimpse of the human side of Paul in his letter to the Galatians. Again, he is writing to churches he had founded in a broad region called Galatia, but this time instead of sharing words of joy and thanksgiving, Paul blasts the recipients of the letter with his anger and disappointment. He has received word that other missionaries have visited the region in his absence, and he is upset that his pupils are foolishly following the misguided teachings of those other people. Paul's pride is hurt and he feels the need to defend his authority against the usurpers. His sense of betrayal is clear when he laments:

> I am astonished that you are so quickly deserting the one who called you in the grace of Christ and are turning to a different gospel—not that there is another gospel, but there are some who are confusing you and want to pervert the gospel of Christ. (1:6-7)

He even declares in anger, "I wish those who unsettle you would castrate themselves!" (5:12). Now, that's not something I would expect a loving Christian to utter, but I can certainly imagine myself feeling the same way!

Disagreements Among Early Christians

So, who were these rogue missionaries who were "perverting" the gospel message? Their exact identity has been lost to history, but clearly they were Christians and quite possibly even followers of Peter or James, two disciples of Jesus and co-founders with Paul of the Christian Church. Fervent disagreement among good people of faith, it turns out, has been with us since the beginning. There truly is nothing new under the sun.

The argument in this case concerned whether Gentile converts to Christianity must be circumcised. James and Peter said yes, but Paul disagreed. Although he was Jewish himself, Paul felt a special concern to preach to the Gentiles and he strove to remove any obstacles to their full inclusion in the new church. As he often does, Paul bases his argument firmly on theological grounds: If circumcision is still required, then that denies the sufficiency of Christ for our salvation, "for in Christ Jesus neither circumcision nor uncircumcision counts for anything; the only thing that counts is faith working through love" (5:6).

I can easily unite with Paul's call to lay aside the circumcision requirement, but I can also see how his passionate convictions hindered his ability to communicate effectively with those who believed otherwise. In practically the same breath that he says "neither circumcision nor uncircumcision counts for anything," he also rebukes, "If you let yourselves be circumcised, Christ will be of no benefit to you" (5:2). That threat, a direct contradiction to his statement that circumcision doesn't matter, would only inflame his listeners further and intensify the discord. How many times do I let my strong emotions get in the way of communicating clearly and thoughtfully in a manner that others can hear?

When I read Paul's letter to the Galatians, I am reminded that disagreements among Christians are nothing new. In some substantial sense, they may even be essential to our survival. The search for God's Truth and God's will for our lives is a never-ending journey. We need to be challenged, prodded, and tested from time to time. None of us has access to the full truth; we sincerely need each other. This reality is the basis for the Quaker decision-making process as well as for our use of clearness committees. However, as children of God we should try to face our conflicts in a loving, respectful manner, realizing that our "opponent" may very well be speaking with God-given authority. We often fail at this task, and I am grateful that the humanity of Paul shines forth in his letters, along with his wisdom.

The Written Word

Paul also reminds us in Galatians how important face-to-face communication is as we strive to work through our differences: "I wish I were present with you now and could change my tone, for I am perplexed about you" (4:20). Written words can communicate only in part and at times may even distort the intended message. Genuine relationships and personal experience are necessary for more complete understanding. I find in Paul's letter a reminder that I cannot find meaning in the words of scripture apart from the context of my own living relationship with God. As Quakers have affirmed since our beginnings, it is the Spirit of God, not the written words in the Bible, which is the source of all truth and knowledge.

Still, the Bible is an unsurpassed record of humanity's relationship with God, and Friends have always upheld the importance of reading and learning from scripture. Unfortunately, too many of us get our Bible in snippets and sound bites. I am a firm believer that, especially for the letters of Paul but also for the rest of the Bible, we should read whole books as a unit and not just a few verses taken out of context. Only in this way can we begin to see the primary messages of scripture and not get caught up in "proof-texting," or attempting to prove our ideas correct by ferreting out verses where "the Bible says so."

Paul and Women

Looking at the big picture is also how I deal with those few verses that for some reason bother me. Take, for example, this difficult passage in Paul's first letter to the Corinthians:

Women should be silent in the churches. For they are not
permitted to speak, but should be subordinate, as the law
also says. If there is anything they desire to know, let them
ask their husbands at home. For it is shameful for a
woman to speak in church. (14:34-35)

In the margin of my worn copy of the Bible is a comment I scribbled when I first read those verses a dozen years ago: "God, you didn't say that, did you?" I had not yet learned how to read the Bible critically as well as reverently, but this passage struck me as totally out of character with the God I knew. Looking at Paul's letters in their entirety is how I reconcile my experience of God and my deep appreciation for scripture with specific words that seem to be so clearly wrong.

I know some Friends read such passages and angrily label Paul a sexist white male, even a misogynist, and for that reason ignore most of his writings. Others try to build a case that Paul didn't really write these words, that they were added by later editors or copyists. I find neither of these solutions necessary nor acceptable. We don't have to dismiss Paul nor find a convoluted way to justify ignoring these words. Rather, we can read them in the context of Paul's entire written record.

Earlier in his first letter to the Corinthians, Paul gives instructions regarding proper attire in church: "Any man who prays or prophesies with something on his head disgraces his head, but any woman who prays or prophesies with her head unveiled disgraces her head" (11:4-5). Clearly, Paul expects women to speak in church, a practice he does not condemn as long as the women wear head-coverings. Even more significantly, Paul praises many specific women in his various letters, women such as Chloe (1 Corinthians 1:11), Phoebe (Romans 16:1-2), Prisca (Romans 16:3-5, 1 Corinthians 16:19), Junia (Romans 16:7), and many others. In each case, Paul praises these women as important workers for the Lord and makes no distinction between the women and the men in the church.

Instead of criticizing Paul for making some remarks derogatory towards women, I try to remember the culture in which he lived and worked. Society at that time was extremely patriarchal and women were often regarded as the property of their husbands. Then along comes Paul, declaring in his letter to the Galatians, "There is no longer Jew or Greek, there is no longer slave or free, there is no longer male and female; for all of you are one in Christ Jesus" (3:28). And in 1 Corinthians, he discusses marriage at length and describes it as a mutual relationship rather than a one-sided one: "The wife does not have authority over her own body, but the husband does; likewise the husband does not have authority over his own body, but the wife does" (7:4). "The unbelieving husband is made holy through his wife, and the unbelieving wife is made holy through her husband" (7:14). Paul challenges some basic assumptions in his society about the relationship between men and women. Far from being a traditionalist, he is actually a revolutionary.

Friends have long insisted that women and men are equal in all respects. We can look to Paul for evidence that sexism is a human convention and not part of God's plan for humanity. Paul was way ahead of his time in his understanding of women's equality, even if he was not as advanced as we might hope him to be. The overwhelming weight of the evidence regarding Paul's treatment of women demonstrates, in my opinion, that he was fair and egalitarian. I find it easy to forgive him when he slips back a time or two into the conventional thought of his day.

Christian Arrogance

Although I have been a Quaker all my life, I have not always been a Christian. Perhaps my biggest obstacle to becoming a Christian was what I understood as the Christian claim that there is only "one way" to God. For years, I rejected Christianity because I felt it was arrogant and disrespectful for me to deny the validity of other faiths. Finally, I could no longer reject the love that I felt Jesus offering me. There were no strings attached to that love, no requirement that I denounce other faiths. I simply accepted the reality of the Living Christ and found myself on the path labeled "Christianity." I've been on this path for over a decade now and never once questioned that this is where I belong.

At first, I proceeded on blind faith that there was, somewhere, a solution to the problem I had with the Christian claim of supremacy. Little by little, I came to understand that it is not my problem after all. It is only one of the myriad paradoxes that come with our faith. Two apparently contradictory statements can both be true, as

Jesus tried to teach us. The last is first, and one must give up one's life in order to live. The reign of God is both now and not yet. Instead of declaring, "Either you are a Christian or you will not know God," I freely affirm, "I believe both that Jesus is helping everyone to find God, and that people can find God without knowing Jesus."

I'm convinced that Paul understood the paradoxical nature of Christian faith and tried, as a pastor, to help others learn to live with the questions instead of demanding easy answers. He doesn't issue one-size-fits-all edicts, but rather molds his guidance to the needs of individual people. For example, in Galatia some members of the church were overly concerned with observing the Jewish laws. Paul exclaims in his letter to them, "Christ redeemed us from the curse of the law" (3:13), emphasizing that adherence to the law will not bring about our salvation. Then in 1 Corinthians he tackles the opposite problem, believers whose behavior has gotten too lax. He admonishes the Christians in Corinth to act appropriately, asserting that "obeying the commandments of God is everything" (7:19). Different situations call for different responses.

Jews and Gentiles

Nowhere is this flexibility as evident as in Paul's treatment of the differences between Jews and Gentiles. As one of the earliest Christian missionaries, Paul lived in a time of significant tension between Jewish Christians and Gentile Christians. A Jew himself, Paul is often referred to as the missionary to the Gentiles. However, he speaks to both Jews and Gentiles in a manner that is respectful and understanding. He encourages Jews to uphold their traditions and obey their laws, but he argues that Gentiles are not obligated to follow the same practices. In short, Paul understands that there is more than one path to God. In his letter to the Romans, Paul writes that "all who are led by the Spirit of God are children of God" (8:14). He does not build walls of exclusion nor demand litmus tests. I find in Paul's words a Friendly tolerance for diversity and even a hint of universalism. He does not flinch from proclaiming his understanding of the truth, but at the same time he makes allowances for those in different circumstances.

Paul's letter to the Romans is unique in that it is the only one written to a church community which he had not founded. It is also likely one of the last letters he wrote before his death. His thinking has matured, and perhaps because he is writing to an unfamiliar group he takes more care to explain his theology. In this letter, we can find substantial evidence that Paul understands paradox to be part of the Christian faith. He doesn't pretend to understand everything, but rather exclaims that God's judgments are "unsearchable" and God's ways are "inscrutable" (11:33). We cannot understand how God works so we needn't concern ourselves with the riddles.

Paul also addresses the issue of Christian arrogance in this letter. In Chapter 11, he discusses at length the plight of Israel. He compares the Jews to the roots of an olive tree, and Gentile Christians as branches grafted onto the rootstock. Paul says to those branches, "Do not boast . . . . Do not become proud, but stand in awe" (11:18-20). The branches are no better than the roots, and in fact could not exist without the support of tree's foundation. He goes on to declare, "All Israel will be saved" (11:26), but without specifying that all Jews will accept Christianity. Jew and Gentile are different, but the difference does not matter in the end.

The Importance of Community

In a similar way, Paul teaches us about the variations among individual Christians. He gives us the wonderful metaphor of the Church as the Body of Christ and each believer as a different part of that body (1 Corinthians 12:27, Romans 12:5). Every member has a unique role, but none is superior to another. All are necessary for the body to be healthy and whole.

I find Paul's image to fit beautifully with the ideal of a Quaker meeting, especially an unprogrammed meeting with no paid staff. We all truly depend on one another and cannot function if a part is missing. From sitting on the facing bench to teaching First Day School, from cleaning the meetinghouse gutters to paying bills or visiting the homebound, all roles are equally vital. Yet each person has been given different gifts, as Paul explains, so that an individual who has a gift for hospitality need not feel guilty for avoiding service on the finance committee, and a person who arrives early each Sunday to pray for the gathering meeting need not feel obligated to clean up after a pitch-in meal. We are wonderfully different, but at the same time we are equally important members of the same body.

Much like many present-day Quakers, Paul places more emphasis on community harmony than on correct doctrine. In acknowledging the different paths of Jews and Gentiles, Paul teaches that the true guide for our behavior is love, not dogma. While the Gentiles he addresses in his letter to the Romans are not obligated to follow the Jewish dietary laws, he admonishes them to be considerate of those who do: "Nothing is unclean in itself; but it is unclean for anyone who thinks it unclean. If your brother or sister is being injured by what you eat, you are no longer walking in love" (14:14-15). Once again, love is the foundation of all relationships.

Guidance for Friends

Paul advises the Romans, "Those who eat [certain foods] must not despise those who abstain, and those who abstain must not pass judgment on those who eat" (14:3). If my monthly meeting felt the need to write a minute on vegetarianism, I could easily imagine our words sounding almost identical to this statement of Paul's. We would want to acknowledge the differences among us in a loving and respectful way. More significant issues among Friends, such as our use of the Bible, our understanding of Jesus Christ, and our different forms of worship, could also be viewed in this manner. We should not let our personal convictions become stumbling-blocks to others. (Romans 14:13) Being part of a loving, accepting faith community is more important to most Friends than having identical beliefs.

It might be a bit of a stretch, but I also find in Paul's writings support for the Quaker view of the sacraments. We generally reject the outward sacraments such as communion with physical elements and water baptism, holding instead that these are inward experiences of our connection with God. Paul makes a point about the ritual of circumcision that resonates with me: "Real circumcision is a matter of the heart—it is spiritual and not literal. Such a person receives praise not from others but from God" (Romans 2:29). What truly matters is what is in our hearts, known only by God, rather than our outward observances.

I am deeply grateful for the knowledge and insights I have gained since I first began reading Paul's letters. No, Paul doesn't write about the teachings of Jesus but, more importantly, he lets his life speak about those teachings. Paul demonstrates by his actions that love is more important than doctrine, that women are equal to men, and that we must be willing to live with paradox. The letters of Paul can be a source of deep inspiration and valuable guidance for Friends if we read them with an appropriate attitude.

The Big Picture

Paul was a real person, just as imperfect as me, which means that despite all my weaknesses and faults I should continue to work for the Kingdom of God as he did. The real Paul did not pretend to have all the answers. I truly doubt that Paul would have wanted others to accept his words as infallible and universally applicable. He reminds all of us, "For now we see in a mirror, dimly, but then we will see face to face. Now I know only in part; then I will know fully, even as I have been fully known" (1 Corinthians 13:12).

Finally, we need to look at the big picture, at the whole of Paul's writings, rather than place too much emphasis on just a few sentences. We need to keep in mind the historical context in which Paul wrote, and separate his own writings from those of others who wrote about him or wrote in his name after his death. We also need to remember that it is the Spirit of God, and not the printed words on the page, that is the source of all truth and wisdom. If we read Paul in a spirit of love, generosity, flexibility, and thanksgiving—just as Paul modeled for us—then we can hear God's voice speaking to us today.

> *Our competence is from God, who has made us competent to be ministers of a new covenant, not of letter but of spirit; for the letter kills but the Spirit gives life. (Romans 3:5-6)*

Deborah L. Shaw is a recorded minister and a member of Friendship Friends Meeting, North Carolina Yearly Meeting (Conservative). Deborah has served her monthly and yearly meetings as presiding clerk, recording clerk, and on a variety of committees. In 2003, Deborah completed the two-year spiritual nurturer program with the School of the Spirit. Spiritual expression in art, music, and literature is of particular interest to her. She is Worship and Discernment Coordinator/Assistant Director of Friends Center at Guilford College where her responsibilities include overseeing the spiritual formation year of the Quaker Leadership Scholars Program and working closely with the worship life on campus.

Do Everything in Love

Deborah Shaw

Speaking as one Conservative Friend among many, from one Conservative yearly meeting among three (Iowa, North Carolina, Ohio) is a somewhat daunting task—except that I can speak only for myself.

Personal Context

Years ago a Guatemalan refugee lived in our home for a while. When he was asked almost any question about himself or his circumstances, he would begin the answer by saying, "I was born in a small village" and proceed from there to set the context necessary for the questioner to understand, as completely as possible, how the answer that he would eventually get to, fit into and was formed by his life story. So when I say that I can only speak for myself, it seems that the briefest outline of my own context might be helpful.

My father is a generational Quaker—my mother a convinced Friend. The marriage of that newly convinced enthusiasm and the steeped-in pattern of a particular (if not to say peculiar) way of being combined to make a sturdy foundation for me. My mother had been raised in the Disciples of Christ, with a Quaker grandmother that we children knew for a time before her death. My mother taught us Bible stories and songs at First Day school, along with Quaker applications of spiritual truths and social testimonies. As a young family we shared daily devotional time, which included reading the Bible. My father's father was raised amongst Conservative Friends in Iowa, and when he married he lived southwest of Philadelphia with his Quaker bride. These grandparents met at Olney Friends School, under the care of Ohio Yearly Meeting (Conservative). Many of my family, myself included, attended Olney. While experiencing a grounding of Conservative Quakerism in the home it was mixed with meeting life as experienced in Philadelphia Yearly Meeting, Intermountain Yearly Meeting, and Pacific Yearly Meeting throughout my early years. Attending Olney for my last two years of high school affected me profoundly, if only realized in retrospect. I moved to Greensboro, North Carolina the fall after I graduated from Olney and have lived there ever since. I started attending, and later transferred my membership to, Friendship Meeting, which had only recently become a member of North Carolina Yearly Meeting (Conservative). Rich in Quaker history and indeed in Quakers, the area I live in has exposed me to the spectrum of Friends through Friends General Conference-affiliated Piedmont Friends Fellowship and the three yearly meetings represented in North Carolina, and through the unceasing stream of notable Quakers who visit Guilford College to share their own experiences of being a Friend. My work at Guilford College and my call to ministry amongst Friends keeps me in regular contact with this wide variety, even beyond North Carolina. While I could say that I am conversant with the spectrum that Friends encompass, it would be right to say that I experience the deepest resonance with the Conservative Quaker expression that I find in North Carolina.

Conservative Friends in North Carolina

As I have traveled amongst Friends I have become aware that many Friends, even those who have moved around in the wider circle of Friends, are sometimes unaware that Conservative Friends exist or, if they have heard of them, are not quite sure what elements distinguish them from the other branches of Friends in the United States.

Conservative Friends conserve the old form of worship—Christ-centered, expectant waiting upon the Lord in open (unprogrammed) worship. In my conservative yearly meeting, North Carolina, one of the most important aspects of our annual sessions is sharing about our spiritual condition with each other. This is done casually and informally over meals and between sessions. Additionally, significant portions of our business sessions are devoted to reading aloud, in a spirit of worship, each of our eight monthly meeting's answers to the twelve complex queries found in our discipline. Each query is read and then the answers are read, followed by waiting worship. Quite often in the margins of open worship someone will testify to the Lord at work in the answering of the query in a particular meeting—or speak to how hearing a particular answer in the session has moved them or brought clarity or brought to light a new way of looking at an issue. Similarly, the state of the society reports from each monthly meeting are read in the face of the meeting, with open worship surrounding them.

Epistles are sent between the three conservative yearly meetings—which speak to, and gently query about, how Truth is prospering among us. Travel minutes, coming back into use generally among Friends in the United States, have never gone out of use in the conservative yearly meetings. Both the epistle and travel minute are opportunities for one body of Friends to convey greetings and prayers to another body of Friends, perhaps with specific references to issues that are known to be in question at the time. All this is by way of saying that the letter format of 1 Corinthians feels familiar to me as a Conservative Friend. It is a letter written by a member and an acknowledged elder of a faith community to a "local meeting."

Query answers, state of the society reports, travel minutes and their endorsements, and the epistles sent and received from the other yearly meetings are all doors into understanding the spiritual condition of our religious society. What resonance I feel or understanding I gain from such communications deepen me in wisdom, in compassion, in opportunities to uphold the members of my faith community in prayer.

The Bible is <u>About</u> the Word of God

A few years ago Friend David Eley was leading the Bible study at our yearly meeting sessions. His theme was, "Christ in you, the hope of glory," and he took us through the New Testament, sharing the passages that speak to this condition of "glory" or "oneness with God." In my notes from his study I have the following detail: a 1920 religious census (presumably in the United States) described

Conservative Friends as not hearing the Bible referred to as the Word of God. This descriptor had resonance for me from the teaching I received in my home and from the witness of Friends along the way. Also in my notes from David's Bible study: To read the Bible as core, but not as the Truth. There are many truths in it, but wait for the Truth to be revealed as you read it. The Bible is not the Word of God; it is about the Word of God. Reading the Bible will help the Truth be revealed to us.

Receiving in the Spirit

What I have been taught and what I have believed to be the "Quaker" approach to reading the scripture is to receive it in the Spirit in which it was given forth, described more eloquently in the excerpt below from section 19.24 of Britain Yearly Meeting's *Quaker Faith and Practice*:

Friends related that understanding of their faith to the scriptures, but they grounded their faith on the Spirit which had given forth the scriptures. George Fox at Nottingham in 1649 was listening to a minister who told the people that the scriptures were the touchstone and judge by which they were to try all doctrines, religions, and opinions, and to end controversy. Now the Lord's power was so mighty upon me, and so strong in me, that I could not hold, but was made to cry out and say, "Oh, no, it is not the scriptures," and was commanded to tell them God did not dwell in temples made with hands. But I told them what it was, namely, the Holy Spirit, by which the holy men of God gave forth the scriptures, whereby opinions, religions and judgments were to be tried; for it led into all Truth, and so gave the knowledge of all Truth.

So much is this my understanding, so embedded in this way am I, that I remember feeling quite disturbed at a Quaker conference where some were presenting their understandings of Quaker theology. Not at the content of the papers themselves, but that the structure of the conference was such that we were receiving the work as just that, work—intellectual academic formulations which seemingly set aside the notion of continuing revelation— and that we, as gathered recipients, were not given the space to receive them in the same Spirit that presumably inspired them.

My approach to reading scripture is rooted in the context described above, whether I am reading it as an individual or studying it with others. When I read the text as an individual, my prayer is that I would be immersed in that same Spirit which inspired those who wrote it, and so receive in that Spirit what I need for the day. I tend to engage the text in a contemplative way, reading and re-reading a portion, resting with it, and observing what word or phrase rises to the surface to instruct, comfort, or challenge me in my present condition. This is not a conscious selective process to purge out the difficult or unpalatable bits of the scripture. Rather it is to allow Spirit to present to me what I need to help me draw closer to God, to resist the pull of the culture that demands that I turn anywhere but to God. I offer up the same prayer when I engage with the text in study, reading commentary and other resources, as well as in discussing the text with others.

Resisting the pull of the culture

The pull of our culture is something that I struggle with on a daily basis. On one hand, it is a challenge to be aware of and sensitive to the myriad subtle and not-so-subtle ways in which the worldly culture impinges on me. On the other hand, it takes courage and ideally companionship to withstand culture's pull and enter meaningfully into the radical lifestyle that God is calling us to. Part of the culture's seduction comes in the guise of asking us to believe that there is no mystery that can't be understood or de-mystified through our intellect or effort. I find companionship and encouragement in the scripture—in standing in and loving the mystery. For the purposes of this chapter, I will be looking at 1 Corinthians as a whole piece—as the letter that it is. Chapter 2 contains one of the major themes of the letter: that the Gospel is the power of God, not a story, and that this power is available to us today. In Chapter 2 of First Corinthians the following verses speak particularly to this.

> My message and my preaching were not with wise and
> persuasive words, but with a demonstration of the Spirit's
> power, so that your faith might not rest on men's wisdom,
> but on God's power. ... No, we speak of God's secret
> wisdom, a wisdom that has been hidden and that God
> destined for our glory before time began. ... This is what
> we speak, not in words taught us by human wisdom but

*in words taught by the Spirit, expressing spiritual truths
in spiritual words. (2:4, 7, 13)*

Receiving God's wisdom through the Spirit

Throughout 1 Corinthians comes the refrain that tells
me that God's wisdom is not the wisdom of the world—
that anyone can receive God's wisdom through the Spirit.
This speaks to me very particularly as someone who works
at an institution of higher learning and yet does not
consider herself an academic. It encourages me in standing
in the truths that have come to me through the Spirit in the
face of co-workers who demand proof and written sources.
It strengthens me in faithfulness when I am led to actions
that seem crazy in the eyes of the worldly culture in which
I find myself. I recognize myself in the phrase; "I came to
you in weakness and fear, and with much trembling"
(2:3)[1].

I recognize the condition of my country when in
speaking of God's wisdom, the passage declares, "None of
the rulers of this age understood it, for if they had, they
would not have crucified the Lord of glory" (2:8). And as I
understand "the least of these" to be Christ—then we are
daily in the business of crucifixion.

The following passages also speak to the power of the
Word—as received in the Spirit—which is available to all
and is not subject to the wisdom of the world:

---

[1] The New International Version of the Bible is used for the
scripture quotations. Except when otherwise noted, all
quotations are from 1 Corinthians.

For Christ did not send me to baptize, but to preach the gospel — not with words of human wisdom, lest the cross of Christ be emptied of its power. ... Where is the wise man? Where is the scholar? Where is the philosopher of this age? Has not God made foolish the wisdom of the world? (1:17, 20)

Yet even with this wisdom received through the Spirit, the author cautions the readers against the temptation to take pride in this gift or to take profit by it — rather care must be taken to remain humble and in the Spirit, even if it means that "To this very hour we go hungry and thirsty, we are in rags, we are brutally treated, we are homeless. We work hard with our hands. When we are cursed, we bless; when we are persecuted, we endure it; when we are slandered, we answer kindly. Up to this moment we have become scum of the earth, the refuse of the world" (4:11-13). The author speaks of this again in 8:1-3: "We know that we all possess knowledge. Knowledge puffs up, but love builds up. The man who thinks he knows something does not yet know as he ought to know. But the man who loves God is known by God." As I read these passages I restate them as queries, "Do I bless those that curse me?" "If I am slandered, do I answer kindly?" "In what spirit do I view those who are homeless, persecuted, and ill-treated?" "Am I able, in humility, to stand with those who are oppressed?" "Am I able to lovingly employ what gifts of wisdom I have received?"

Spiritual Gifts

Spiritual gifts, membership in the Body of Christ, and an understanding of ourselves in spiritual community are important concepts presented in this letter to the Corinthians. If not the exact place, this surely is one of the places that early Friends got their understanding of how we are all ministers, variously, one to another. "There are different kinds of gifts, but the same Spirit. There are different kinds of service, but the same Lord. There are different kinds of working, but the same God works all of them in all men" (12:4-6). At times amongst Friends I have felt a division between those whose gifts are manifested more outwardly and those whose gifts are manifested more inwardly. Here is a reminder of how all the gifts are needed—in their fullness—to accomplish God's purpose for our meetings. As we are able to stand in unity, in community, in the body, our potential is increased. That potential is not just about the happy workings of an insular, isolated faith community. It is from the cohesive, spirit-led community that miraculous transformative works of service to the world can be sustained.

Chapter 12 lays out how the gifts given are sufficient to the needs of the community. In verses 22-26 we are told that

> *those parts of the body that seem to be weaker are*
> *indispensable, and the parts that we think are less*
> *honorable we treat with special honor. And the parts that*
> *are unpresentable are treated with special modesty, while*
> *our presentable parts need no special treatment. But God*
> *has combined the members of the body and has given*

greater honor to the parts that lacked it, so that there
should be no division in the body, but that its parts should
have equal concern for each other. If one part suffers, every
part suffers with it; if one part is honored, every part
rejoices with it. (12:22-26)

Here the query that surfaces is "Have I made an effort to see, understand, and give thanks for the many quiet and subtle gifts that come together in the life of my meeting?" This way of regarding our interactions and being can be carried outward to our other places of community.

A portion of the letter on "orderly worship" also has resonance for me in understanding and approaching our meeting for worship. Paul spends some time here talking about the gifts of prophecy and of tongues. I recently learned (and then learned that most people I shared it with already knew) that the word "prophecy" means to speak on God's behalf, not just speaking about something that would be happening in the future. The author begins this section:

Follow the way of love and eagerly desire spiritual gifts,
especially the gift of prophecy. For anyone who speaks in a
tongue does not speak to men but to God. Indeed, no one
understands him; he utters mysteries with his spirit. But
everyone who prophesies speaks to men for their
strengthening, encouragement and comfort. (14:1-3)

This points toward the value of sharing with one another our various experiences of God's workings in our lives in order to build up the church and strengthen the body. Later in this passage comes the instruction: "When you come together, everyone has a hymn, or a word of instruction, a revelation, a tongue or an interpretation. All of these must be done for the strengthening of the church" (14:26). In other words, we are all ministers and must do our part in creating healthy worship. Our part may be sitting silently and upholding all present in prayer and so manifest one of the less showy spiritual gifts mentioned earlier—yet this is equally crucial to the well-being and growth of the faith community as is the vocal ministry.

Also found in this section is a difficult passage about women—that women are to be silent in the churches—not allowed to speak. How am I to understand this passage when earlier the author speaks about women praying and prophesying with no question but that this is right and natural? To speak to this, I can go to commentaries which explain about how this is a particular letter to a particular community and therefore this section is not a universal edict; that "speaking" is markedly different than "praying" or "prophesying;" or share the view that I recently heard that some of the more misogynist views seen in the letters of Paul do not correspond with his overall tone or the sentiment expressed in Galatians 3:28 ("There is neither Jew nor Greek, slave nor free, male nor female, for you are all one in Christ Jesus"). However, it is most truly in my own heart, where Christ's spirit daily writes the law, that I find the answer and I hear that I am asked—that we all are asked—to speak on God's behalf. I also recognize that I am a product of my own particular context in this, but am not out of line with my own faith tradition, stated in last part of the quote from section 19.24 of Britain Yearly Meeting's *Quaker Faith and Practice*:

It is significant that Fox, after justifying women's meetings by abundant quotation from scripture, concluded with the words: If there was no scripture... Christ is sufficient.

Watch Over One Another for Good

Throughout this book, the good of others is lifted up. Following the admonition against spiritual arrogance is the promise of the gentleness with which readers might expect to receive God and further instruction about how we should be caring for one another. In 4:20-21, the author states "For the kingdom of God is not a matter of talk but of power," and questions "What do you prefer? Shall I come to you with a whip, or in love and with a gentle spirit?" In later parts of this letter there are cautions to those who are "in Christ" to behave in exemplary ways so that the witness of their lives does not cause someone watching them to stumble on the spiritual path.

In the Advices and Queries of North Carolina Yearly Meeting (Conservative), I hear echoes of this concern when we are enjoined to "let our whole conduct and conversation be such as becometh the Gospel" and to "exercise ourselves to have a conscience void of offense toward God and toward all persons."

Daily, my life witnesses to those around me. To what am I witnessing? To God's love and presence in my life? To my own fascination and surrender to the culture in which I am embedded? "Nobody should seek his own good, but the good of others" (10:24). As Paul closes this first letter to the Corinthians, particular care is requested for those traveling in the ministry. I feel myself in this same stream, having listened to travel minutes being read which commend the traveling Friend to the loving care of the hosts. I have traveled under such minutes and have known experientially the love and concern that both carried me forward and received me.

The Greatest of these is Love

For me, the central theme of this book is captured in the thirteenth chapter which is certainly among the most well known of all scripture—a beautiful and flowing treatise on the nature and properties of unconditional love—and an acceptance of standing in the mystery represented by that. This chapter follows the chapter on spiritual gifts and is prefaced by the following sentence: "And now I will show you the most excellent way."

> *Love is patient, love is kind. It does not envy, it does not boast, it is not proud. It is not rude, it is not self-seeking, it is not easily angered, it keeps no record of wrongs. (13:4-5)*

While this amazing passage is often read at weddings, the ideal of love expressed here is not just for lifelong partners, but for each one of us to attempt to realize in all our relationships. We are given instruction in how we might achieve this ideal in the following description of love:

> *Love does not delight in evil but rejoices with the truth. It always protects, always trusts, always hopes, always perseveres. (13:6-7)*

Here again we are asked to stand against the surrounding and dominant culture which most clearly demands that we answer anger with anger, violence with violence, and hatred with hatred. This "most excellent way" is asking us to act and react from the place where perfect love casts out fear. The first three verses of the thirteenth chapter refer to the spiritual gifts detailed in the previous chapter and state clearly that without this love these gifts are as nothing, and their expression is devalued without the accompaniment of a loving spirit and intention. This seems most clearly expressed in the following verse:

> If I have the gift of prophecy and can fathom all mysteries
> and all knowledge, and if I have a faith that can move
> mountains, but have not love, I am nothing. (13:2)

In the section that begins with "Love never fails," I hear an echo of the warning that worldly wisdom does not make us wise—that God's wisdom is received through the Spirit—and that even the spiritual gifts that impart wisdom will be seen as partial in the fullness of time and coming of God's kingdom. If our words, actions and deeds are motivated by Love—Perfect Love—then they will always be for the good of others.

The closing paragraph in the Advices found in the North Carolina Yearly Meeting (Conservative) *Faith and Practice* reads as follows:

> Finally, dear Friends, let your whole conduct and
> conversation be such as becometh the Gospel.
> Exercise yourselves to have a conscience void of
> offense toward God and toward all persons. Be

faithful and steadfast in your allegiance and service to your Lord; continue in His love, endeavoring to keep the unity of the Spirit in the bond of Peace.

This is an echo, an amplification, of the encouragement offered by Paul as he closes this first letter to the Corinthians:

Be on your guard;
stand firm in the faith;
be men of courage;
be strong.
Do everything in love.
          (16:13-14)

Do everything in love.
The place to begin and the place to end.

Beckey A. Phipps is a member of Fresh Pond Monthly Meeting (Cambridge, Massachusetts), New England Yearly Meeting. She has a graduate degree in theology from the Episcopal Divinity School in Cambridge. She completed the School of the Spirit program (Philadelphia Yearly Meeting), "On Being a Spiritual Nurturer." She offered the Bible Half-Hours for New England Yearly Meeting and for the Annual Gathering of Friends General Conference. She has served Friends General Conference as the clerk of the Religious Education Committee and is presently the clerk of the Traveling Ministries Committee. She also served as the Coordinator of the Boston-area Quaker Studies Program and has led retreats and workshops among Friends.

Beckey has been employed in church administration since 1998. Her recent publications have covered mysticism and social transformation, the spirituality of institutions, religious education, and Bible studies. Beckey and her long-time partner, Tania, live in Massachusetts.

(Photo by Joanne Clapp Fullagar)

FINDING HOPE IN EPHESIANS

Beckey A. Phipps

*I pray that the God of our Lord Jesus Christ, the Father of
glory, may give you a spirit of wisdom and revelation as
you come to know him, so that, with the eyes of your heart
enlightened, you may come to know what is the hope to
which he has called you. (Ephesians 1:17-18)[1]*

A Brief Summary of Ephesians

The epistle, attributed to Paul, but probably written by
a follower as much as a generation later, was not
specifically addressed to the church in Ephesus. It
appeared in its earliest-known copies to be a circular sent
to a number of the early churches. In it, the author
described God's *mysterious plan* for the salvation of *all*
believers, uniting Jew and Greek (Gentiles, or Greek-
speaking pagans, who became Christians) into one
body/church. That plan was "set forth in Christ as a plan
for the fullness of time, to unite all things in him, things in
heaven and things on earth" (Ephesians 1:9-10). With the
eyes of the heart enlightened, the author prayed, the
converts would come to see that this unity with God and
each other was the hope to which they were called (1:17-
18). The epistle warned that hostilities between Jewish and

---

[1] All biblical references are from the New Revised
Standard Version.

Greek converts threatened to alienate them from God and each other. But grace, the gift of God, would unite them in one whole structure, the church, with Christ as the cornerstone—and this would be the dwelling place for God (2:21-22).

In the series of ethical exhortations that followed, the converts were begged to live lives that would "make them worthy of their calling" (4:1) as saints. The member/body analogy employed by Paul in earlier epistles was also used here—the faithful were to become "members of one another" in the body of Christ (the church). In that relational way of being, they would be "imitators of God" (5:1) living in love together, "as Christ loved us" (5:2). The members of the church, like members of a household, were to be subject to one another as they were subject to Christ (5:21-6:9). Lastly, the converts were urged to "be strong in the Lord" and put on "the whole armor of God" to resist the evil powers of the world (6:10-17).

Where I Am About the Bible

> Rather than loud, settled slogans about the Bible, we might do better to consider the odd and intimate ways in which we have each, alike and differently, been led to where we are about the Bible. (Walter Brueggemann)

I am not in a settled place with the Bible, and my reading of the epistle to the Ephesians, in fact, leaves me quite unsettled. I don't find the experience of being unsettled necessarily a negative one. I continually and earnestly feel challenged to explore my experience of God, and God's claim on me, whenever and wherever I engage with the Bible. While I may search for firm ground to stand on in my relationship with God and the biblical community, I am well aware, also, that having a settled place to stand can lead to idolatry and close-minded pride. If everything were settled then I would, without doubt, limit the boundless mystery of God in my heart and mind—and grow deaf to the continuing revelation of the Truth.

I feel compelled to offer the reader even the briefest of explanations of the "odd and intimate" journey I have traveled to this moment of reading the epistle to the Ephesians. Like any other Bible reader, I bring to this reading my interpretation—a lifetime of experience, woundedness, yearnings, assumptions, and education. I cannot separate myself from my circumstances, my identity, and my self-understanding; they channel my approach and my comprehension. Bible scholar Walter Brueggemann affirmed that there is no other honest way to come to our interpretation of the Bible, for the Bible invites us in our very particularity to engage with the God who is revealed in its pages.[2] I have found, in fact, that the Bible offered the most wisdom to me when I read from a place of unsettledness, or openness and questioning. I imagine this is what has made the Bible's wisdom enduring for generations of readers.

---

[2] Walter Brueggemann, William C. Placher, and Brian K. Blount, in *Struggling With Scripture*, (Louisville: Westminster John Knox Press, 2002), 13.

I approach the Bible as a complex person who has traveled a complicated journey toward Christianity. Two significant aspects of who I am factor into my reading of Ephesians and I reveal them because they are essential to my reading—critical to my interpretation. They provide me with a hermeneutic born of my life experience. I am a lesbian feminist Quaker. I am aware that this declaration of some portion of who I am, a sexual minority and a feminist, may give some readers of this book reason to pause at this chapter. In our present era of very great and anguished controversy about gender roles, same-gender marriage, and the backlash against feminists, I risk being misunderstood and dismissed, at the least. I am fully and painfully aware that minority sexual identity and sexually immoral behavior are not legitimate distinctions for many Bible readers. I acknowledge, furthermore, that feminism is experienced by many as an essentially hostile or oppositional philosophy.

It would be reasonable of the reader to wonder if I approach the Bible with hostility. I admit that I certainly have felt hostile, guarded, and bewildered, as well as amazed, humbled, examined, broken open, consoled, and instructed. All of these emotions and experiences came into play in taking up Ephesians. As I describe my reading of Ephesians, I humbly ask for the good faith and charity that members of the biblical community can hope for when they come to the table together, with openness to hearing another's experience—perhaps an openness, even, to the point of unexpected conversion.

For others, my statement of identity will be an explicit reason to read this chapter, as they may seek some place to stand in their own unsettledness with the Bible. The verse from Ephesians (1:17-18) that is quoted in the heading suggests that there are insights and wisdom available that can open the eyes of the heart to the promise of God through the witness of Jesus. Through the example of Jesus' actions in the God-gathered community we may feel the hope that we are called to and through which we may find our heart's desire—to be welcomed and affirmed in our whole selves in the blessed and thriving community. To be affirmed in wholesome communion with the mystery that is God the Creator.

The author of Ephesians claimed that followers of Jesus were members one of another, joined by God into one gathering, or circle, with dividing walls torn down and hostilities ceased (2:13-14). I share with you my persistent question, "When people have been alienated from each other over many bitter years, is that still possible?" The Bible narrative reveals affirmative answers. Yes, this is the *promise of God;* it is evidenced in the history of the Israelite community, and through the transforming actions of Jesus.

What follows is a description of some of the situations and surprising conversions that led to my earnest and provisional reading of the Bible—and the epistle to the Ephesians. Though what I offer is not the very beginning, nor even the whole story, it is a good place to start.

My Road to Ephesians

In the early 1980s I attended a music festival for women. Thousands of women gathered on hundreds of wooded acres in Western Michigan and enjoyed the talents of musicians, comediennes, storytellers, and craftswomen.

Living and playing together in community, it was a time of celebration. We were vibrantly and affirmatively ourselves without the usual social and behavioral constraints women feel in the presence of men.

One balmy evening I went with some friends to set up our camp chairs in front of the concert stage. Once seated, I began to look around me at the other "festi-goers" with an enjoyable, relaxed curiosity. Every concert was another opportunity to marvel at the wildly varied, creative appearances and behaviors of women who felt the safety and freedom to be themselves. Close-by were two young women seated on a blanket on the ground. I had to look twice to be sure of what I saw them doing, because I was so astonished. They were reading the Bible.

This was certainly one of the more surprising behaviors I had encountered at the festival. And I confess I did not react with charity or even bare tolerance. In some significant part, that was because one of the formative religious experiences of my young adulthood was having a professing Christian thrust the Bible in my face and tell me that I should die because of what he said was God's judgment of lesbians. He seemed absolutely gleeful at the prospect of my damnation and eternal suffering. Many of my friends had had similar threatening experiences, many of them within their own families and churches.

So there in the midst of thousands of women, nearly all of whom were lesbians, were two women reading the Bible—a symbol of much condemnation, oppression, and tragedy. For millennia, church communities had found words within its pages to justify the humiliation, hatred, and condemnation of women, as well as sexual minorities and enslaved peoples. On that August night, in the lush fern-covered woods of Michigan, I felt very deeply and personally the thunderous clash of two worldviews. In my experience to that point, one of these worldviews felt loving, affirming, and justice-seeking—and the other felt hateful, alienating, and death-dealing. The biblical worldview was the latter.

Seven or eight years after that memorable experience, ironically, I found myself searching for an alternative church or spiritual community. I heard that lesbians and gay men were welcome at Red Cedar Friends Meeting in East Lansing, Michigan. I went to my first meeting with virtually no knowledge of the Religious Society of Friends and the biblical foundations of Quaker faith, worship, and testimonies. What I did know was thirst. I was thirsty, very thirsty, for deep, contemplative communion, and that meeting, based in silent, waiting expectation, was a "long, tall drink of cool water"—though it surely felt strange at first. Gradually overcoming my shyness and guardedness, I found hospitality, love, nourishment, and a new way of being. As I came to inhabit the deep world of Quakerism, I felt less alien and more at home.

In addition to becoming an active member of the meeting, I ventured out into the wider Quaker community and crossed paths with Friends who knew the Bible well and embraced its lessons and mysteries. In varied settings among Friends I worshiped with lesbians and gay men, feminists, intellectuals, contemplatives, and activists who related God-revealing stories from the Bible with a spiritual humility that disarmed my long-standing defensiveness. Most memorably, I recall Friend Elizabeth

Watson and her vivid, poignant stories of the women around Jesus. Elizabeth had once been publicly ostracized by an organization of Quakers and denied the opportunity to speak before them because of her friendship and alliance with lesbian and gay Friends.

In 1991, after hearing Elizabeth at the annual Gathering of Friends General Conference, I was moved to purchase a Bible. I was forty years of age. I felt a strong measure of embarrassment and suspicion, because internally, I still felt the reverberating clang and clash of intersecting worldviews. This was one of a series of unexpected conversions in the process of my convincement as a Friend, in the process of moving from estrangement to communion with the community of God.

When I began this long, eventual journey leading to Ephesus, I was not literate in the Bible, nor even a fluent Quaker. Though I was brought up a cultural Christian (nominal observance on major holidays!), I was not raised in a circle of people who were conversant in the Bible. For the Bible to become an adopted language for me, I felt its witness must resonate with the quiet, persistent presence of God I had long experienced in my unschooled, natural condition. So, I did not sit right down with my new Bible in 1991 and read it from cover to cover. It felt too enormous and dangerous a project. I needed wise, imaginative teachers and guides to help me learn how to approach the text and see the wondrous ways that the Spirit would be revealed within it.

Just four years after hearing Elizabeth Watson, I entered the Episcopal Divinity School in Cambridge, Massachusetts. I went to learn more about those Bible stories of the women in Jesus' circle. I went to consider their experience and their testimonies of the in-breaking of God in their lives—as far as was possible for me in my growing understanding. I went to take up the interpreter's task, hopefully, with imagination and academic rigor. Most of all, I needed a place to take my curiosity and yearning for convincing, lucid responses to my urgent questions about the Bible and Christianity—questions that reflected my experience of feeling embattled by the beliefs and practices of biblically-oriented persons who have been my neighbors.

Those particular questions were not theoretical or academic; they reflected very compelling, personal pastoral needs. In order to overcome feelings of alienation from the biblical community, I needed to understand why the God-given value (esteem) and agency (freedom) of women had been so callously, even brutally, treated in so many biblical accounts. I knew that some of those deeply unsettling stories and messages had the long-term effect of robbing women's lives of hope.

Was it, for instance, really acceptable to the biblical community when Lot offered his daughters to be gang-raped by a mob, rather than that he might be considered inhospitable to male angels? (Genesis 19:1-14). Why was the name of the woman who anointed Jesus in Mark's gospel (14:9) forgotten, when Jesus was so confident that she would always be remembered? If Jesus taught that all were beloved of God without distinctions and social assignments, an insight the apostle Paul claims to have received, then why were wives/women subject to the husband/male head of the Christian household, as the epistle to the Ephesians asserted? (5:22-24).

Hadn't Jesus established relationships with women that reflected the reality of God's true social order where women were not treated as inferiors, and where there was no second-class status at the shared table? Hadn't Jesus encouraged Mary, Lazarus' sister, when she was drawn away from *setting* the table toward *sitting at* the table and enjoying the companionship among the other disciples? And wasn't Martha's resentment of her sister equally telling? Perhaps she had the insight that if the work was shared by all, in a discipleship of equals, then all could have sat down together as equals. Was that the hope to which Martha was called? (Luke 10:38-42).

Some will claim that such a questioning, critical reading of the Bible demonstrates how I insert my contemporary feminist self into the text. This is true. I do read the Bible from my immediate, very personal perspective and search for the wisdom of the scriptures—like all other readers. My reading is informed by knowledge of the long-term, real-time price that has been paid by women and others of low status resulting from the persistence of patriarchal readings of the text. Great tragedy has resulted from such readings, and one of those tragedies has been the outright rejection of the Bible and its sacred wisdom. But what I could not know earlier in my life was how the text, how Christ Jesus, would eventually begin to *question me.*

Having laid out some of the landmarks along my road to Ephesus, I will now turn to the critical message in the epistle that captured the promise of unity through the transforming love of God. I will also consider the insertion of a behavioral code that demonstrated a limited human vision of the ordering of God's household, one that contributed to the failure to realize the hoped-for unity and, instead, ended in untold numbers of broken hearts, bodies, and spirits across the millennia.

The Epistle to the Ephesians: A Plan for the Fullness of Time

The first dimension of gospel order was/is living in a way that nurtures and maintains the covenantal relationship with God. (Sondra Cronk)

In my reading, the primary message in Ephesians is that God, through the radically reorienting actions of Jesus, extended an invitation to all the faithful to become members of the covenantal community of God's household. The early Christian community, gathered by God, was united in an experience of the transforming power of that good news of God's all encompassing love. The terms of the covenant, so plainly articulated in the actions of Jesus, were that the members love God wholeheartedly and love one another as they were loved by their Creator (Mark 12:29-31). A new order of being could be realized on earth where this covenant was lived and practiced faithfully. The community of the gathered was a holy, dwelling place of God—the church (Ephesians 2:21-22). That was God's plan to be realized in the fullness of time, which Jesus asserted was at hand (Matthew 10:7; 12:28; Luke 10:9).

The divisions and hostilities that historically divided the Jewish Christians and Greek Christians were to be laid to rest in the fully realized peace of Christ, a peace achieved through priorities *re-ordered in heaven*. The Gentiles were now welcome at the table, though once they were "aliens from the commonwealth of Israel, and strangers to the covenants of promise, having no hope and without God in the world" (Ephesians 2:12). The provisions for being members in good standing of the church (community, household, or gathered circle of God) were that they act (that their lives witness) like a people (saints) transformed through love and that as members of God's community they be subject to one another (in a discipleship of equals).

This mysterious plan, or movement, of God to unite the faithful had been unfolding and developing in the progress of centuries leading to the First Century circumstances of the recipients of the epistle—and wherever believers were gathered in a circle of faith and worship. It was certainly God's prerogative, and the biblical pattern, to renew and reframe the covenantal promise, to gather the once excluded, to enlarge the circle, according to the circumstances of the Israelite community in particular times and places. Moses explained at Sinai, for example, that the covenant God made with them in their time of exile was not the one made with their early ancestors (Deuteronomy 5:3).

Among the very particular covenantal stipulations voiced by Moses, for instance, was the exclusion from the temple of those men with unwholesome (repugnant or damaged) sexuality and foreigners (Deuteronomy 23:1-8). Yet centuries later, as shown in Isaiah 56:2-8, those particular covenantal terms were completely re-ordered during the restoration of the Israelite community after the Babylonian exile. In that specific time the struggling community was reconstituted and its self-understanding was reframed within a story that revealed who exactly *were* the faithful persons in that worshiping community, among them Sabbath-keeping eunuchs and foreigners (who likely married into the community).

The terms of inclusion/exclusion in the covenant made at Sinai with Moses' community was subsequently modified in Isaiah to include eunuchs and foreigners. These persons who were once, without doubt, misunderstood, outcast, and treated with hostility by the core community then became honored members, very particularly welcomed to God's community in the conditions of a new covenant. The foreign believers were embraced so conclusively, in fact, that they were allowed to become priests, the most exclusive of all categories among the Israelites. It was on this occasion that the author of Isaiah 56 declared that God's "house shall be called a house of prayer for *all* peoples. Thus says the Lord God, who gathers the outcasts of Israel, I will gather others to them besides those already gathered" (56:7-8).

Jesus referred to this passage in Isaiah 56 when he entered the temple in Mark 11 and was outraged at the sacrilege he encountered there. "Is it not written, 'My house shall be called a house of prayer for all the nations'? But you have made it a den of robbers" (Mark 11:17). I read this as another example of Jesus' affirmation of the continuing expansion of God's community. The sin that outraged him was not the increasing diversity of the faithful gathered at the temple during the Passover season, but the *unjust exploitation* of the faithful by those who profited at their expense.

Moving far forward in the history of Christendom we come to another small sect of witnesses in the unfolding, mysterious plan of God. The Quakers in the seventeenth century, and beyond, considered their experience and condition similar to that of the early Christian communities, such as the Ephesians, the Romans, or the Corinthians. They also were a *gathered people*, drawn into unity by God and with each other through the restoring and transforming experience of the gospel of Jesus. They understood themselves, in fact, to be *primitive Christianity revived*, welcomed by God into a new covenantal community. The covenant of their very particular experience, written in their hearts by the *indwelling* Christ Jesus, led to radically re-ordered lives in a time of great civil and religious upheaval in Western Europe.

The Quaker understanding of "gospel order" referred to the manifestation of this new covenant in every aspect of their communal worship and living, and by extension, that "new order would affect all of creation, restoring all things to their right relationship with God and each other."[3] In George Fox's vision that meant restoration to the very newness of God's creation, to the *time before the fall*, before Adam and Eve's disobedience in Genesis 3:16,

---

[3] Sandra L. Cronk, *Gospel Order: A Quaker Understanding of Faithful Church Community.* (Wallingford, PA: Pendle Hill Publications), Pamphlet No. 297, 5.

when humanity thrived in its original unity with its Creator.[4]

In the twenty-first century, I have witnessed the circle of God expanding yet again, and the gathered community of the New Jerusalem reassessing the varied identities of those who are numbered among the faithful. What was condemned in a scant few biblical texts as exploitive, immoral homosexual behavior between heterosexuals does not add up to condemnation of authentic intimacy between same-gendered persons. This important distinction is critically nuanced by our contemporary understanding of an inherent sexual differentiation in a minority of the population. A difference, in my experience, that reflects the unfathomable diversity of God's creation. We who were once uniformly cast out, shamed, and despised, are now, through increasing insight and compassion welcomed as equal, faithful, and beloved members in God's community—though far from everywhere and not in all hearts.

As I have shown, this challenging shift in the inclusiveness of the faithful is not unique in the history of God's widening community. We can, however, infer from our own anguished experiences in the present how the acts of exclusion were suffered in the past. Jesus' actions of love and welcome for all despised peoples is a transforming message of grace from the God who gathers. The exhortation in Ephesians that we bear with one another in love, "making every effort to maintain the unity of the

---

[4] George Fox, *Journal*, John L. Nickalls, editor, (Philadelphia Yearly Meeting, 1985), 27.

Spirit in the bond of peace" speaks clearly to the present gathered community's divisions. Let us reaffirm the covenant of faith by turning *away* from idolatry, dishonest cruelty, violence, and the exploitation of human beings (and all of creation) and by turning *toward* obedience to the Light, which calls us to love.

The Household Code

> Who established the division between the genders in their many historical expressions? Why have these men and women who need one another established a hierarchy based on their bodies and started a kind of war in their relationships? (Ivone Gebara)

I find one of the greatest of tragedies for humankind is the ordering of human relationships according to strength, perceived superiority, gender, and race. These hierarchies have led, and continue to lead, to divisions and wars—not only in the mass scale of great armies clashing in war, but also in the persistent, mass scale of psychological, spiritual, economic, and physical battles between intimates. In my reading, Jesus was quite clear about human and heavenly ordering: those who are first on earth shall be last in God's community (Matthew 19:30; Mark 9:35).

The great hope that I feel in reading the first four chapters of Ephesians is held in tension with the anger, frustration, and sorrow that I experience in reading the passage between 5:22 and 6:9. The epistle's one significant flaw was its juxtaposition of the ordering of an ideal Greco-Roman patriarchal household with that of God's household. In my experience, this human ordering has

clay feet and has resulted in *dis*-unity and exploitation—
with lasting, bitter alienation between men and women,
children and parents, those who enslave and the enslaved.

In the passages from Ephesians 5:22 to 6:9, known as
the *household code* (also found in Colossians, 1 Peter, 1
Timothy, and Titus) the epistle established specific terms
of relational behavior for members of the household. The
early Christian churches were located in private houses
and, as such, were "house-churches." The early
theologians, like Paul and his followers, found the
authority of the church/Christ over believers as analogous
to the authority of the patriarch over the members of the
household. Many current biblical scholars and general
readers interpret the relational ordering of the household
code as an indication of the early church communities'
attempts to conform to the pervasive patriarchal society
around them, and, thus to reduce the persecution they
suffered because of their egalitarian, communal, counter-
cultural practices—modeled by Jesus as the way of
transformation.

Sarah J. Tanzer, a religious historian of Judaism and
Christian origins, has reported, however, that
Mediterranean households were not uniformly and largely
patriarchal. Independently wealthy and self-sufficient
urban women, for instance, had become more common
and accepted as householders in the Roman Empire.[5]

---

[5] Sarah J. Tanzer, "Ephesians," in *Searching the Scriptures: A
Feminist Commentary*, edited by Elisabeth Schussler
Fiorenza (New York: Crossroad Publishing Company,
1994), 330-331.

Tanzer, and other biblical scholars, have asserted that the roles of such women (as well as those of household slaves) in the early urban Christian house churches mirrored a culture that was more tolerant of non-traditional households. Paul's relationships with his female colleagues provided evidence of the spiritual authority and leadership of certain notable, faithful women. Some within the early church communities, however, were determined to identify the Christian movement with more conservative traditions, over and against liberalizing trends that had gained acceptance in the wider imperial and pagan Roman culture.

Tanzer posited, therefore, that the entire household code may have been "dropped in" at a later date by a redactor (an editor with a theological agenda) for the purpose of reigning in Christianized women, children, and slaves who felt liberated from their lower social status and restrictions. Verse 5:21 followed the behavioral exhortations to *all* the members of the church and concluded, simply, that members be subject to one another *without any ordering according to status*. With verse 22 that equality among all subjects is supplanted with a hierarchy of subjects. The addition, while in beneficent language, insinuated the inferior position of wives to their husbands, children to their fathers, and slaves to their masters in the church of Christ. And it clearly linked the authority of *paterfamilias* (male head of household) with the authority of Christ.

Though I have cited scholars and historians in my interpretation of Ephesians, this is no academic or philosophical matter for me. It is, again, a pastoral issue based on my life experiences. Tanzer's hypothesis is squarely situated in the growing historical evidence that the early Christian communities attracted and nurtured non-traditional followers, and that a slow degradation of Jesus' radically inclusive community began within decades of Paul's death.

The patriarchal ordering of family, social, and political life was and remains tenacious and oppressive. The historical reality of those whose lives exist on the lower levels of the household/social order, with decreasing levels of power and privilege, has been one of chronic, sinful misuse and injustice. The shameful experience of those who are the subjects in the household code is that the unity in the church is maintained when such members know and accept their places. This is the result of a hierarchy of human-created values, with self-gratification at its heights and abuse at its depths. This is not the hoped-for outcome in a God-gathered circle with heavenly-ordered values.

A Hopeful Conclusion

I feel assured, with the writer of the epistle to the Ephesians, that there *is* a "mysterious plan" of God *to gather up all* in the fullness of time. It is a plan that even my meager experience of the Spirit of Wisdom and Revelation affirms is continuing to unfold—even as I know that the faithful only possess limited pieces and visions of that divine plan. In what may be incomprehensible to the community, and has certainly been actively resisted, those once outcast from God's sight in other eras and places have subsequently been seen to be gathered up. In spite of a biblical witness of God's ever expanding reach and Jesus' deliberate inclusiveness at his table, there remain divisions, misunderstandings, and hostilities among the disciples—all of which continue to threaten alienation from God and one another.

I will always wonder what might have been the alternative outcome of centuries of reading the Greek scriptures if there had been no stratifying of subjects in the Household Codes. What richness of spiritual experience, wisdom, and prophecy might the subjected peoples have brought to the development and leadership of the church? What more might we have glimpsed of the mystery of God in our neighbor if our eyes were lifted to each other, on the level, rather than cast downward in subjection and humiliation?

The hope that I am called to, what the eyes of my heart envision as a woman and a sexual minority, is that the circle of those gathered will continue to expand through the renewing grace of God. In every heart and in every era, God communicates the invitation that can lead to the realization of this hope. I have felt myself personally welcomed to, and situated in, the circle of Bible-reading Quakers. My experience gives me hope in the unity to which we are called, to dwell with God and one another close in a holy place—no longer divided and dividing, no longer foreign to one another, but in a discipleship of forgiven and forgiving neighbors.

Somewhere out there are two Bible-reading women whose paths I once crossed many years ago in Michigan...

Bibliography

Brueggemann, Walter, William C. Placher, & Brian K. Blount. *Struggling with Scripture.* Louisville: Westminster John Knox Press, 2002.

Cronk, Sandra. *Gospel Order: A Quaker Understanding of Faithful Church Community.* Pendle Hill Pamphlet No. 297. Wallingford, PA: Pendle Hill Publications, 1991.

Dunn, J.D.G. "Ephesians." In *The Oxford Bible Commentary,* edited by John Bartman and John Muddiman, CD-ROM, 68. London: Oxford University Press, 2001.

Fiorenza, Elisabeth Schüssler. *Bread Not Stone: The Challenge of Feminist Biblical Interpretation.* Boston: Beacon Press, 1984.

Fiorenza, Elisabeth Schüssler. *In Memory of Her: A Feminist Theological Reconstruction of Christian Origins.* New York: The Crossroad Publishing Company, 1990.

Fiorenza, Elisabeth Schüssler. *Discipleship of Equals: A Critical Feminist Ekklesia-logy of Liberation.* New York: The Crossroad Publishing Company, 1993.

Perkins, Pheme. *Ephesians.* Nashville: Abingdon Press, 1997.

Tanzer, Sarah J. "Ephesians." In *Searching the Scriptures: A Feminist Commentary,* edited by Elisabeth Schüssler Fiorenza. New York: Crossroad Publishing Company, 1994, 325-348.

Trevett, Christine (ed). *Women's Speaking Justified and Other Sventeenth-Century Quaker Writings about Women.* London: Quaker Home Service, 1989.

Watson, Elizabeth G. *Wisdom's Daughters: Stories of Women around Jesus.* Cleveland: The Pilgrim Press, 1997.

White, L. Michael. *From Jesus to Christianity: How Four Generations of Visionaries and Storytellers Created the New Testament and Christian Faith.* New York: HarperCollins Publishers, 2004.

Born in 1935, John Punshon has outlived communism and fascism and never succumbed to the charms of phenomenology, existentialism, or deconstruction. He received a literary and classical education at his English grammar school and Oxford University, and is, therefore, immune to the charms of untested innovation.

He spent most of the 1970s acquiring the rudiments of theology and biblical criticism. In 1979, he became Quaker Studies Tutor at Woodbrooke and afterward was Professor of Quaker Studies at the Earlham School of Religion.

In the 1980s, Punshon encountered non-theist modernism which, he concluded, was an unwarranted inference from the central Quaker tradition. In trying to assess its significance, he came to see universalism, pluralism, non-theism, and experiential-expressive religion as the inevitable consequences of postmodern ways of thinking.

In the subsequent decade, he came to acknowledge the limitations of modernity, and to see revelation as the only reliable source of knowledge of God. He thereby came to reclaim the evangelicalism of his childhood that has always been implicit in his writing, and was subconsciously what he has always believed.

He is a member of Whitewater Monthly Meeting and a recorded minister in Indiana Yearly Meeting. His favorite things include *The Magic Flute*, Gray's *Elegy*, catfish, *Persuasion*, West Ham United, daffodils, art deco, Ricky Skaggs and the *Drudge Report*.

MISS WILSON'S LEGACY: HOW MY EARLY SCHOOLING TAUGHT ME TO READ THE LETTER TO THE HEBREWS

John Punshon

I have never been of the opinion that accuracy is the same thing as truth. More than half-a-century ago, I was privileged to have been taught by Miss Wilson in my primary (grade) school. I remember where our classroom was, and I know she taught us for two years, but the rest is entirely hazy apart from a few odd memories. But Miss Wilson's influence on me has been profound. It was she who told us stories—national epics, Greek, Roman and Norse myths, folk tales, and of course, the Book. I knew the parables and the sequence of events in the Old Testament by heart by the time I was eleven, and in modern jargon, my role models were set out for me. I had an idea about what was right and what was wrong, what conduct was acceptable and what wasn't, what personal virtues and qualities I should aim at, and above all, *why*. I am entirely incapable of understanding what a secular education must be like.

Miss Wilson was part of Wales' greatest export to England apart from coal—teachers. Unless she was not true to type, she was probably a clever lass who grew up in the Valleys and got a scholarship to a grammar school and then teachers training college. Her folks were either miners or in the coal trade, and were probably part of the great Welsh revival of the 1900s that gave us, among its many gifts, the magnificent hymn tune *Cwm Rhondda* (look it up in your hymnal). In all probability, she was chapel and not church, as the saying went, that is, a Methodist. She had the faith in her bones, and she helped to transmit it to me. I have loved the scriptures ever since Miss Wilson opened them to me.

I have no reason to suppose Miss Wilson had read Albert Schweitzer or knew about form criticism or neo-orthodoxy. She may well have, of course, but I doubt if that sort of thing was of much interest to her. Much later on, it was necessary for me to learn that the nature and date of the Exodus was debatable; a number of different people wrote the Psalms; the sequence of events in the gospels had a didactic and not a historical purpose; and Paul did not write all the letters traditionally attributed to him (like the Letter to the Hebrews, as it happens). Miss Wilson never told us the Bible has inconsistencies, nor that it is made up of sources from very different periods of time, nor that the text is a palimpsest, showing many different editorial revisions and emendations.

Nor would it have been right for her to do so, because this sort of thing would have been beyond my fellow pupils and me. Cognitive and emotional development take place together, and while they can be facilitated, they cannot be hurried. An adult worldview is the development of a childish one, not a substitute for it, and we were at the earlier stage. The point is, religion is about our worldview, not just what the conventional wisdom tells us about this and that. Miss Wilson, I hope, understood I would derive infinitely greater benefit from the characters and the stories she told us than any other method that would have asked us to be, even in the smallest degree, critical.

So, under Miss Wilson's instruction, the Bible came alive to me, and has remained so all my adult life. It is not a text with which I wrestle nor a resource to which I turn. It is my daily companion and guide; it tells me things I need to know but cannot discover on my own. When people call the Bible "the Word of God" this is what they are trying to convey—the medium and the message are somehow special, and the message of the Bible is unlike, and cannot be reduced to, any other form of communication. I want to take the Letter to the Hebrews as an illustration of these principles because I have always been specially drawn to it, and its teaching has a direct bearing on the message of the early Friends.

In what follows, I begin with a description of what the Letter is about and the place it occupies among the New Testament writings. It is a very ancient document of course, and there are problems in reaching an understanding of it. The middle part of my essay is a discussion of how we constitute the meaning of religious texts and makes the claim that this analysis is a necessary preliminary to assessing what truth, and therefore authority, they might be said to possess. It follows (I argue) that the distinction between primary and secondary forms of religious knowledge is untenable, and calling the Bible a "secondary" authority has led over time to many Friends not regarding it as an authority at all. Consequently, we need a willingness to look again at what we have always taken for granted, with a sympathetic, but nevertheless critical eye.

Towards the end, I will discuss the influence of the Letter on the formulation of early Quaker doctrine, and conclude with a reprise of my argument that narrative (an external reality) is as essential to the discernment of religious truth as personal conviction. This is where the authority of the Letter, and therefore the validity of early Quaker claims about the nature of the Church, actually reside. Webster defines revisionism as "advocacy of revision, esp. of some authoritative or generally accepted doctrine, theory or practice." This is an essay in revisionism, so you need to be forewarned—I have my doubts about the adequacy of George Fox's attitude to the Bible.

Summary of the Letter

The Letter to the Hebrews dates from the period between the crucifixion and the destruction of the Jerusalem Temple in 70AD. In these years, the emerging Church faced three tasks: (a) to give reasons for its claim that Jesus Christ was the fulfilment of the promises in the Hebrew Scriptures (b) to meet the challenges and criticisms of its message that inevitably followed and (c) to work out the implications in its message that were not immediately apparent. Each of these matters is touched on in the Letter, and it gives us a fascinating insight into the mind of the Church at the very earliest period of its development.

The Letter has a simple aim: to explain the uniqueness of Christ. Taking his divinity for granted, it seeks to portray his life and works as the fulfilment of the precedents and prophecies of the Hebrew Scriptures, and the life of the Church as a continuation of the story contained in these already ancient books. What distinguishes the two periods in question is God's action in changing the basis of his relationship with his chosen people. Hitherto, his commitment to them and theirs to him (the Covenant) was expressed in an institution (the Temple), an organization (the Priesthood), and a set of regulations (the Law). One participated in the covenant by the offering of sacrifices for various purposes, notably for the forgiveness of sin. Christ, however, had offered himself, once and for all, as a sufficient sacrifice for all the sins of the world, now and yet to come. A new covenant had come into being.

To have meaning and to carry conviction, therefore, the Letter has to show there is continuity between the old and the new covenants, as well as providing reasons for the superiority of the latter one. Logically, it stands or falls on the nature of Christ's sacrifice. Is this an act of God or not? If not, then there are no compelling reasons for adopting the new faith. If so, the sacrifice is unique, and the consequences the Letter draws are inescapable. The Old Covenant has been superseded by a New Covenant. Its argument cuts two ways. In one direction, it gives an interpretation of the Hebrew Scriptures, which it hopes will convince. In the other, it makes specific claims, based on the crucifixion and the resurrection as matters of historical fact.

Underneath the first-century argumentation, there is an attempt to locate religious reality in personal experience and not efficacious ritual, and the argument carries weight on the assumption that the Christian extension to salvation history is factual. Consequently, the Letter carries out a reinterpretation of the institutions and practices of the old covenant. Christ is the High Priest, but his advocacy is in heaven, not here. His sacrifice is eternally sufficient and unrepeatable. The covenant is an inward reality, fulfilling the prophecy of Jeremiah 31. The place of worship is no longer the earthy Temple, but the dwelling-place of God. Our access to the sacrifice is no longer membership of the cultic community, but through faith and the community of the faithful. The last few chapters in the Letter describe what is involved in the life of this community of faith, the Church.

How I use the Text

The Letter, then, is about sin, sacrifice, priesthood, faith, and other conceptions, which draw their meaning from the spiritual world of the first century.

There will be evangelical and liberal interpretations of the Letter, I suspect, and I know a number of Friends who would read it in what I would recognise as seventeenth-century terms. I don't know which group I fall into. I do not read the Bible as a Friend, a freemason, a freethinker, a food faddist, a football fan, or anything else. The idea would never occur to me. I might be influenced by the fact that I *am* a Friend, but it is *me*, and not my affiliation, that is doing the reading. I certainly read as a member of a community, but that primary community is rather older and larger than the Religious Society of Friends.

In practice, the Bible is a constant companion to me, and I use it in worship, in personal prayer, in theological reflection, in deciding matters of doctrine which exercise me, and for spiritual formation; though actually, *I* don't do that—God does it to me. Scripture is, by far and away, the most important influence on my life. Let me take five texts from Hebrews that illustrate this general process, and then go on to see how they reflect a deeper set of presuppositions about the meaning of the Letter and thence the scriptures as a whole.

In Worship

First, there is worship. Whenever I attend public worship, these words are present or not far from my mind: "Therefore, since we are surrounded by such a great cloud of witnesses, let us throw off everything that hinders and the sin that so easily entangles, and let us run with perseverance the race marked out for us" (Hebrews 12:1)[1]. The verse is important because of its historical associations. While reflecting Paul's image of the Christian life as a race requiring personal discipline and devotion, it also conveys a profound sense of belonging. My worship is always conditioned and directed by the great cloud of witnesses, whose presence I feel. These words were written in the very earliest years of Christianity, and it should be borne in mind the word translated here as "witness" is actually "martyr" in the original Greek.

---

[1] Except as noted, scripture references are from the Letter to the Hebrews in the New International Version of the Bible.

In Prayer

Second, there is prayer, which to me is the articulation of a personal relationship rather than a form of reflection or meditation, though these also have a place in my religious life. We read, "since we have a great high priest who has gone through the heavens, Jesus the Son of God, let us hold firmly to the faith we profess... Let us then approach the throne of grace with confidence, so that we may receive mercy and find grace to help us in our time of need" (4:14-16). Jesus, of course, tells us to offer prayer in his name, and this text clearly explains why. Once, I used to pray in my own strength, adding the formula "through Jesus Christ our Lord." I didn't know why. It seemed a nice way to end. Now that I understand why the Holy Spirit is described as our Advocate, I have come to understand that Christ stands at my side as I pray and lends his strength to my words.

In Theological Reflection

Third, there is theological reflection. Theological reflection can reinforce our prejudices by confirming our desires; it can confine itself to our intellect and break the link with faith; or it can be the vehicle of a continually deepening understanding. The choice is ours. The Letter is written from faith and purports to convey spiritual truth. "Now faith is the substance of things hoped for, the evidence of things not seen" (11:1-3). These words seem to me to represent a challenge to intellectual discernment, enquiring exactly what we hope for and what evidence we accept for the nature of the spiritual realm. I prefer not to take this verse out of context and generalise from it. Rather, I examine my faith in terms of the doctrinal framework of the Letter as a whole, which lends meaning to these words. The verse is like a Query, because it asks whether my understanding of the truth is securely based.

In Deciding Matters of Doctrine

So we come, fourthly, to the question of deciding matters of doctrine. "Anyone who lives on milk, being still an infant, is not acquainted with the teaching about righteousness. But solid food is for the mature... Therefore let us leave the elementary teachings about Christ and go on to maturity, not laying again the foundation of repentance from acts that lead to death, and of faith in God, instruction about baptisms, the laying on of hands, the resurrection of the dead, and eternal judgment. And God permitting, we will do so" (5:13-6:3). This is good advice. It is pointless—indeed dangerous—to be preoccupied with the finer points of doctrine, when what matters is to understand their consequences and application. Refining doctrine is not growth in grace; deepening one's understanding of the truth of doctrine *is*.

In Spiritual Formation

Finally, spiritual formation. "For the word of God is living and active. Sharper than any double-edged sword, it penetrates even to dividing soul and spirit, joints and marrow; it judges the thoughts and attitudes of the heart. Nothing in all creation is hidden from God's sight. Everything is uncovered and laid bare before the eyes of him to whom we must give account" (12:12-13). There is an important reminder here. God is the inescapable reality in whom we live and move and have our being. What I understand as spiritual development or spiritual formation—growth in grace, to use the conventional term—is to realise this reality in one's own life. This is not an easy process. Coming to the Light never was. Without judgment there is no reconciliation. Before I can become what God wants me to be, I have to know who I am.

Meaning and Truth

These texts are important to me in a variety of ways. For example, by means of the guidance they offer, they exercise an influence over my conduct by the conditioning they exert. They inform and create a frame of mind out of which my decisions come to be made. In short, they are guides to action. But they go beyond that. The Letter makes claims about God that go beyond personal preference and purport to represent generally ascertainable truth rather than just personal opinion, even at the distance to two millennia. Clearly a process of interpretation is going to be necessary here. What am I to make of a first-century writer here in the twenty-first?

My first task is to establish what he means, and this process is both helped and hindered by the fact that there is no such thing as a freestanding meaning, because things do not have meanings in themselves. Even something as simple as a traffic signal, for example, depends on convention. Society accepts red as meaning "stop!" so we do. The meaning of a red light is just that, a command to do a certain, generally understood thing. (Of course, a red light has another meaning in the *demi-monde*, but that again depends on convention).

Meanings come into being in response to need. What we say on any given occasion is coherent because it fits in with what we have previously said, that is, it arises in a *context*. It is comprehensible to others because it is part of a system of communication that goes beyond ourselves and involves others; that is, it arises out of a set of *circumstances* in which we are not the only player. It is perpetuated by *convention* because to establish meaning all parties rely on a common code, or basis of interpretation. Meaning depends on our being understood, as well as our own desire to be intelligible. Meanings also change with the times. They are conventional, and therefore flexible, and give rise to occasional misunderstanding and confusion. Mostly, we deal with them successfully.

But, they need care. When a word is used in religious discourse, say, "Trinity," "faith," or "repentance," we have to bear two dimensions in mind. One is its place in contemporary speech and the common associations it possesses; the other is the various shades of meaning it may have had over quite a long period of time. Meanings actually go through quite subtle changes, and we have to be sure that we and ancient writers, like the author of the Letter, are using the same conceptions. This is less problematic than it sounds, given reasonable care.

So those who enter into public debate about theological and philosophical matters that have a primary bearing on the practice of religion have a responsibility to understand this. The meaning of a religious statement derives from the context in which it is used and necessarily reflects arguments and controversies that go well beyond the immediate experience of the individual making the statement. It is a commonplace of modern hermeneutics that authors often convey far more than they know or intend, and one of the tasks of criticism is to uncover the assumptions and implications of a passage that might not have been present to the mind of the person who wrote it. The Bible has always been subjected to this kind of analysis, necessarily and properly.

Meaning, while not the same thing as truth, is the essential vehicle by which we come to recognise the truth. We cannot reach it in any other way. We learn the meaning of things from childhood through influences like upbringing, education, personal experience, reflection, and cultural conditioning. This kind of meaning, whatever more it may turn out to be, is first the creature of convention. But there comes a point at which we talk to other people, enter into an intellectual tradition, and begin to formulate a worldview that often goes beyond our early influences, which we learn to qualify, and, indeed, sometimes even to reject. Through meaning, we encounter the problematic idea of truth, which, among many other things, enables us to distinguish knowledge from misapprehension and error.

Finding the truth is not always an easy task, as those who have served on a jury will know. In establishing the truth of a statement or an argument to our own satisfaction, we have to deal with necessary preliminaries like consistency, verifiability, abstraction, variation, and nuance. These are inescapable logical realities, and they take us beyond the personal. They constitute the principle of rationality, and without them intelligent discourse is impossible. If we ignore them, we are left with nothing more than competing monologues or shouting matches. For minds to meet, even to disagree, there have to be some common assumptions about what constitutes knowledge, and how it can be established.

This is a complex, but by no means intractable, problem. Establishing meaning is a necessary preliminary to reaching a judgment about the truth of something, and why that judgment is to count as knowledge. Judgments about truth are usually made in particular cases, often in unique sets of circumstances, yet these judgments are profoundly influenced by wider worldviews, as well as the particular occasions on which they are made. Accordingly, we need to analyse the meanings of these wider structures of thought, because they also have a bearing on what is to count as knowledge. On this basis, the truth is not a litmus paper we use to test the genuineness of a claim, the meaning of which is clear. The truth is in symbiotic relationship with meaning, not independent of it. Both jewels are to be found in the same mine.

Truth and Authority

In the early and formative period of Quakerism, it was customary to distinguish between kinds of religious knowledge according to their origins and methods of reception, namely, the kind of knowledge that came from inner experience and the kind that came from the Bible. The former was deemed more reliable than the latter since it came direct from God and was not dependent on the weaknesses of reason or the vagaries of human experience.

It was also considered more authoritative, for the same reason. In this way, a series of opposites emerges: certain and uncertain, absolute and relative, primary and secondary. These characteristics can be attributed to both particular claims to knowledge and particular means of knowing.

I have difficulty with this way of looking at things. First, I think it rests on a faulty theory of mind. Unless I possess some infallible faculty of discernment, I will use exactly the same mental apparatus to discern both godly and worldly guidance and truth. If I do not possess such a faculty, then all my judgments will be logically of the same status. Second, as I have just attempted to show, the data on which our judgments—religious and otherwise—are made, are too complex to be reduced to such a simple formula. In both cases, what is going on is induction, and we should not be afraid to accept that religious judgments are largely inductive.

One can see how it can be argued that knowledge can be certain, absolute, and primary, but it is hard to see how knowledge can be uncertain, relative, or secondary. The problem with the traditional dualism is, if one allows that knowledge derived directly from God is absolute, one has then to ascribe some kind of status to the non-absolute kind of knowledge that is mediated to us. If what distinguishes it is its origin, then we have no principle for evaluating the many and various truth claims that come from this source; some of which are undoubtedly from God, but some of which, obviously, are not.

As a theory of knowledge, then, this outlook has some consequences I personally find questionable. If a claim to inward illumination is allowed, *prima facie*, to be accepted as genuine, there will be a temptation to proceed immediately to the conclusion that it is genuine, and either neglect or ignore the process of discerning its value.

If a conflict arises between what scripture is believed to be saying and what an individual asserts, there will be a tendency to prefer the voice of individual illumination, and a consequent and unjustified diminution of scriptural authority. Also, throughout Christian history, the principle that to the pure all things are pure has led to antinomianism (i.e., the view that the sanctified cannot sin—even when they perform acts that would be sinful for others), which has always been confined to small sects and has proved of no value whatever in the development of Christian ethics and political theory.

The traditional position is also somewhat limited by its seventeenth-century origins, and it is helpful in this connection to put early Quaker epistemology in some sort of context. It may well be there are varieties of knowledge, as the inward/outward dualism seems to require. But, one might argue the alternative, that one can be acquainted with something without necessarily having comprehensive knowledge of it. If this is so, instead of postulating different kinds of knowledge, as traditional Quaker theory seems to require, one might propose there is one kind of knowledge, but we have varying degrees of confidence in our formulations of it.

Probability is nothing more than approximate knowledge, and we have no difficulty in living successfully in a world of probabilities. So, it seems odd to me to demand copper-bottomed certainty when it comes to religion. The influence of Descartes has not always been desirable, and Quakerism, traditionally, has been a Cartesian religion. But is Descartes the best we can do today? I think not.

The second reason for my revisionism is, granted the complexity of the process of verification, we should be very chary of claiming certainty in it. I am reluctant to accept philosophical certainty for religious statements, because to do so is to diminish the importance of faith and open the way for all those dangerous trends the early Friends correctly recognised in the churches of their day.

Conclusions

There is no doubt the magic (or grace) that charmed me as a child and drew me to the scriptures, was the stories they told. I would think Miss Wilson's attitude was that the big picture could take care of itself, as long as the children responded to the many smaller incidents and stories that went to make up the whole. If she did think that, she was very wise, and also, very strangely, managed to anticipate one of the major themes of contemporary biblical criticism: that the framework of narrative has a very significant part in the construction of meaning, and therefore, the articulation of truth.

The Letter to the Hebrews draws its significance from an underlying narrative it assumes and partially articulates. I pray and think the way I do because I place myself in this story. I do not read as a critic or an outsider, but as one who participates in the reality it describes. As I indicated earlier, the religious community I was brought up in, and that shaped my whole consciousness, is that which traces a continuous existence back to the teaching of the Apostles as preserved in the New Testament. But, I had at some point to transcend these influences and make the faith my own, to decide not just to remain within the Church, but to decide what kind of Christian I was going to be.

Well, of course, I became a Friend, but that is not much of an explanation without an account of how it comes about that there is a Society of Friends for me to join. This is in itself a part of the narrative. One of the reasons why the Letter is so important to me is that it provides a place for me to stand, a theological justification for the loyalty I have espoused. I first grasped the importance of the Letter to Quaker thought when I read Joseph John Gurney's *Puseyism traced to its Root* (1845), a slim book defending evangelicalism and attacking the Catholic revival in the Church of England. Here, Gurney is repeating the line of reasoning he used earlier in Chapter 4 of his *Observations* (1827) where he defends Friends' disuse of the ordinances by the same means.

In these writings, Gurney argues (fairly conventionally) that salvation is the product of the covenant of grace, which is mediated historically through the preparatory period described in the Old Testament, and the fulfilment described in the New Testament. While the love of God continues, there has been a transformation in our relationship with God because of the death and resurrection of Jesus Christ. The whole basis of worship has been changed because of Christ's sacrifice. No longer is it tied to outward observance, because the realities of covenantal membership are matters of the heart. "For it is by grace you have been saved, through faith—and this not from yourselves, it is the gift of God—not by works, so that no one can boast. For we are God's workmanship, created in Christ Jesus to do good works, which God prepared in advance for us to do"(Ephesians 2:8).

This approach positions the Christian faith in a specific account of human history, which, until the rise of liberal theology, was unquestioned in the Church. There was certainly vigorous debate about the details, but the suggestion this was not part of divine design and control never was. Needless to say, most Christians (including non-theologically liberal Friends) continue to labour under this conviction today, as I am sure most members of my own yearly meeting would.

In Quaker terms, of course, it enables us to square a troublesome circle. On the one hand, we can reasonably claim the plainness and inwardness of Quakerism does not compromise with, and therefore better reflects, the principles of the New Testament (one risks spiritual pride in saying this, of course, but I guess if I *had* to debate the issue, I would be willing to make this case). But at the same time, many of us identify ourselves as evangelicals, and we square the circle because we find the stress on conversion and holiness, which we find among other non-Quaker evangelicals, is something we are very much at home with, and which seems to us to be quite compatible with what we have historically read in the Letter to the Hebrews.

So, the Letter to the Hebrews shows me that God relates to us publicly through a covenant, not just though inward and unmediated private revelations. I have already quoted five texts and described the ways in which they influence me. I read them not coldly, like an unseen translation examination in which I have to decipher the language and construct meaning out of the passage before me. What I find in them is shaped by the knowledge I have about how they came to be composed and the place they have in the history of Christianity. This is not simply a matter of identifying them as "scripture" but to understand they represent a stage in the development of a certain complex of ideas with antecedents and consequences that is at its lowest an aspect of the general history of ideas, and at its highest (as I believe), divine revelation.

The texts presuppose the general framework of the Letter, the theological elements utilised by Gurney are fundamental in different ways in defending the integrity of church against synagogue, Protestant against Catholic, and Quakers against the rest. They are like flesh on bones, and without the ideological or theological skeleton, they really don't mean much; comforting or inspiring though they might be to me personally. The point about meaning is, it is publicly accessible. Debate about meaning is more than competitive self-assertion, where the statement, "it is true for *me*," trumps any other consideration.

Hence, as I have already argued, these texts operate as part of a narrative that is the vehicle of meaning, and therefore carries the prior claim to authority. The texts are embedded in the narrative, and have no independent meaning, except in terms of some contemporary and non-historical theory of what Christianity is; which does not concern me here. Meaning (and we should not ignore the possibility of multiple meanings), arises out of a complex of influences, and each one of them needs attention and analysis. These influences comprise a perceptual and conceptual framework, which we inherit and which defines our thought. The vocabularies we use, and the experiences open to us, arise within this framework.

Not exclusively, of course. It is perfectly possible to accept the analysis of Jewish practice described in Hebrews without accepting Christ as the Messiah. It is possible to accept Gurney's opinion as to its contemporary relevance without accepting the particular Quaker spin he puts on it. The reason, quite simply, is our religious life *does* begin with an inward and unmediated experience. While this experience is described differently in the various historical strands of the Christian tradition, what is being described is obviously the same thing. In terms of the reformed theology from which Quakerism sprang, we experience effectual calling. In the Arminian churches, we encounter prevenient grace. Among Friends, we are convinced by the Light of Christ within. Divine inspiration continues as we grow in grace under the tutelage of the Holy Spirit.

My argument certainly contains the element that unmediated inward experience is a necessary part of religion. It carries an ultimate authority (and is said to be "ultimate"), because our highest duty is to follow our conscience, not some sort of external rule we have voluntarily placed ourselves under. However, three hundred years after the early Friends promulgated the idea that *because* this is the primary authority in religion, the narrative of the faith is therefore secondary, we need to re-examine whether this continues to be an adequate formulation.

The dictionary will tell us "secondary" means belonging to the second class in importance, not primary or original, subordinate, derivative, of minor or lesser significance. My case is that such experiences are necessary, but represent the beginning of a process of developing understanding, which can only be nourished by so-called "external" sources, i.e. the Bible. The Bible provides an explanation of the nature of the experience, the reason for it, and where it comes from; and it provides a corrective to any misstep. It is the corporate dimension that enables the transmission of the truth over many generations; it means we do not have continuously to re-invent the wheel; and it enables progress—not the continual repetition of what we know already. Inward and immediate revelation is, therefore, incomplete and insufficient as it stands as the basis for the life of a community. We are justified, as Friends used to say, to the extent we are sanctified. If there is any truth in that statement, it is because sanctification happens over time. It is the same thing with understanding—there are no short cuts.

Janet L.R. Ross is both a birthright and convinced Friend. She has a Ph.D. in Hebrew Scripture, Ancient Near Eastern History, and Archaeology. Janet has taught classes in Biblical Studies, Comparative Religion, Religion and the Media, and Apocalypticism. She is currently teaching at McMaster University in Hamilton, Ontario.

Janet has written on historical theology and biblical interpretation in such essays as "The Biblical Basis of the Friends Peace Testimony," and "Lifting the Veil: Apocalyptic Imagination in W.E.B. DuBois' The Souls of Black Folk." She has traveled extensively, including the Middle East and South America, exploring the connections between historical and ideological contexts and current world situations and events. She has a special interest in cultural apocalypticism and its relationships with religious teachings.

HIDDEN MANNA, HIDDEN MEANINGS: UNVEILING REVELATION

Janet L.R. Ross

Background Introduction

I was well into my dissertation on the apocalyptic portions of the Book of Daniel before I rather sheepishly realized it was my childhood reoccurring nightmare. Granted, the Bible is not written for children, but still, many of us have come to know the scriptural stories as children—and I have heard throughout my years of teaching scripture that I am not the only one to have nightmares inspired by biblical stories from the flood to David's decapitation of Goliath. While certainly the Bible is a beautiful text in so many ways, it has become important to me to address the whole of biblical scripture and not to leave out a chapter or verse because it is difficult to understand. This has led in part to my interest in the book of Revelation, that final apocalyptic portion that takes themes from Daniel and expands them for the drastic times of the Roman Empire.

Called "deliberately obscure," "grimly lurid," and "blindingly splendid," the book of Revelation both begs for and prohibits understanding. It is this violent and sometimes horrific book that concludes the Christian New Testament canon, yet it continues to invite ongoing interpretation through its imagery and vision. Similar in many ways to other biblical stories of exile and community, the Apocalypse of John, a.k.a. Revelation, is also about exile—what separates us—and about community—what brings us together and binds us together. This type of conflict and resolution is the stuff of all good plot lines in narratives, sacred ones notwithstanding. Because the Book of Revelation has been the source of much divisive controversy and confusion, and because I believe its insight into the nature of "empire" and community is so critical for our times today, I have chosen to write on this text.

First Glance

Before addressing John's Apocalypse specifically, however, allow me to briefly comment on biblical/scriptural interpretation in general. One of the first things I want to know when reading scripture is what the words really mean or, stated another way, what was the point of writing the text the way it is. In our modern Bibles, many Hebrew words remain untranslated into English and, instead, are transliterated. For example, we know that Jesus' birth took place in Bethlehem and that he was laid in a manger. But, knowing "Bethlehem" means "house of bread" and a manger is literally where one "eats" is to know that Jesus' teachings are as primary to life as the main food source of the Middle East, i.e., bread. To locate Jesus' birth in Bethlehem and his first place of existence in a manger is a signal to the hearer or reader about the importance of the teaching that is to come. Such emphasis on narrative detail was common throughout Jewish tradition and is found in other religious traditions of sacred text as well. (Further examples of inherent meanings in biblical names include why Joseph—whose name means "to put"—has problems with "putting" or "placing" and "misplacing" his clothes, etc., why Mary the Magdalene has the same name as Mary the mother of Jesus, and even why Jesus echoes the actions of his namesake Joshua in the Hebrew Scripture/Old Testament.)

Additionally, there are numerous Hebrew and Greek biblical narratives that carry within even their smallest details certain hints and signs which point toward the meaning of the sacred text. (Again, examples include why Jesus wears a seamless robe, why Moses encounters a burning *bush*, and why the number seven is considered to be particularly sacred.) Yet, it is not just the details that we fail to translate or interpret. While many of us know the Hebrew word for "the LORD" is the Tetragrammaton (four letter) יְהֹוָה or YHWH literally translated into English as "I am," most do not realize that it is the Hebrew construction of the stative verb form "to be." This means that the translation is not only "I am," but is also "is," "are," "was," "were," "be," "been." Therefore, we cannot state who we are, where we are, what anything is, without inherently invoking that "God" is at the basis of all that exists, of all that was, that is, and that is to come. See, for instance, Revelation 1:4, 8, "John to the seven churches that are in Asia: Grace to you and peace from him who is and who was and who is to come, and from the seven spirits who are before his throne... "I am the Alpha and the Omega," says the Lord God, "who is and who was and who is to come, the Almighty.""

It is helpful to note two things here. First, Hebrew verb forms are primarily of two kinds, "perfect" and "imperfect." A perfect verb is one whose action is completed. An imperfect verb is one whose action is not yet completed. Because the Hebrew alphabet is written without vowels, the consonants can carry within them both meanings of past (perfect) and present or future (imperfect), leaving the appropriate interpretation up to the reader (or to tradition as the case may be or often is). Second, while the statement "I am the Alpha and the Omega" is often understood in English as "I am the beginning and the end" (referring to the first and last letters of the Greek alphabet), a better translation is that "God" or more specifically "I Am," is the "Alpha *to* the Omega" or from the beginning to the end and all in between. In other words, everything—everything now and everything that has been and everything that is to come. Given this literal translation, perhaps a more accurate name for YHWH or God would be "Is-ness" or "Being."

Similarly, in English the word "god" comes from a verb that means "to call." Consider how this changes a Westerner's theological conception of God; rather than that which *is*, God is that which *we call upon*. Knowing this, it is perhaps easier to understand the assumptions that lurk behind English/Western theology and its emphasis on theism. Recognizing God as that which *exists* within what *is*, rather than viewing God as an "other" upon which we call, might provide us with a new perspective about our irritating neighbors, our exploitation of the environment, or of ourselves.

I keep a saying by my desk, attributed to the philosopher Ludwig Wittgenstein, that admits, "The limits of my language are the limits of my world." In much the same way, knowing the Hebrew and Greek languages behind our English translations (or transliterations) has significantly influenced my own understanding and love of biblical text, theology, and spirituality. On almost a daily basis, I am wonderfully surprised by new challenges to my English vocabulary assumptions. While I am not suggesting that everyone learn Hebrew and Greek (though I admit that would be my ideal), I recommend reading the Bible with the help of a variety of the aids available that help us understand what the biblical writers were trying to say. Certainly, it is unlikely that we, reading centuries after those first audiences, will be able to catch all the intimations, allusions, and nuances that early narrators may have intended. But, even so, there is much that we can learn about the early context, culture, language, and tradition that can only serve to enhance and enrich our understanding and experience.

Second Look

A related issue of concern when reading biblical texts links this emphasis on linguistic/textual meaning with the Quaker emphasis on spiritual experience. While I believe that starting with a historical context is crucial to reading ancient texts, the importance of recognizing the spiritual context should not be underestimated, as it is intimately linked to understanding various meanings within sacred texts. Perhaps it is not out of line at this point to consider *why* we should try to understand the meanings of sacred text, especially ancient sacred text. We can safely assume that text has come to be called "sacred" because it has, in some way, been interpreted as revealing something about the Sacred, something that encourages our understanding of and experience of the Holy. And, within sacred texts, we find passionate and compelling stories that not only speak of mystical, transcendent experiences of the Divine, but encourage such experience for others.

Throughout time, various people (often the ones who eventually become prophets) realized—and continue to realize—that mandates and doctrines do not in and of themselves inspire people to love and compassion. Rather, it is the *experience* of the divine that is truly inspiring, that profound thrill of exhilaration that excites our soul and utterly transforms our understanding of who we are and what it is to be alive. Who would not desire this experience for ourselves and for others? Who would not strive for an experience that brings with it the swell of love and peace that is so desired and desperately needed in the world? Thus, we are left with the problem of how we learn to have spiritual experiences, how such experiences are encouraged, how they are taught.

Quite brilliantly, sacred texts resolve the problem of how to learn about spiritual experience by teaching us through story and narrative. Just as Jesus taught with parables and our parents and grandparents taught with examples from their own lives, we learn through life's "stories." Certainly, too, we live and learn as our own life story unfolds, but when we can learn from another's experience, we can often understand more quickly and deeply something significant about life. Hence, the telling of stories of beginnings and endings, of laughter and sorrow, of fathers and mothers and sibling rivalry and reunions, of governments and community, of truth and beauty. And thus, sacred text is born.

The problem that arises is literally how to make the text one's *own* experience, for knowing words and knowing lived truth are two very different kinds of ventures. In his book, *Essays on the Quaker Vision of Gospel Order*, Lloyd Lee Wilson highlights the Quaker inheritance of knowing things experientially first, before any action is taken, or even before any structured belief is adopted:

> Early Friends described themselves as persons who had undergone a radical transformation—George Fox called it "passing through the flaming sword." Today we often put the cart before the horse, and speak of the testimonies as being at the heart of Quakerism; but our spiritual forebears made no such mistake. They knew "experimentally" what we often forget: outward change and/or reformation are not by themselves sufficient to change human beings even if they were possible by themselves, and they are not in fact possible without a concomitant inward transformation. God's grace and love acting in our hearts is the necessary first motion which makes all other change possible. ... an attempt to adhere to the testimonies alone does not make one a Quaker: one's inner reality is stronger than one's will concerning outward behavior... (pp. 163-64.)

The Hebrew prophets, the Gospel writers, Paul, John and countless other religious figures have said this same thing; namely, that any attempt to adhere to mere words, doctrines, or testimonies alone is never equal to the actual experience. On one level, we understand this clearly. We would never, for example, confuse the word "stone" with an actual stone, or the word "waterfall" with an actual waterfall. (My mother used to tell us, "Listen to what I *mean*, not what I *say*.") Even if I described in perfect detail the reality of fire, it would never be the same as feeling the actual heat and seeing the flaming colors. Yet, throughout our religious history, we continuously confuse words about the divine, about what is holy and sacred, with the actual experience—even to the point of denying our own or others' experience if or when they do not fit the specific chosen words of the time. Sacred text is sacred because it directs us toward God, toward the sacred "Being," not in being God/the sacred itself. Indeed, sacred text has been charged with a difficult and seemingly impossible task— that of teaching us *how* to have a religious experience. I like the metaphor of sacred text as a finger pointing at the moon. If we concentrate only on seeing the finger, we will assuredly always miss the moon.

Third Dimension

This brings us back to the Apocalypse of John, and specifically to the question of what John is pointing us toward. The Greek word "apocalypse," αποκαλυψις, stems from two words: "apo," απο, which means "to lift away from," and "kaluptein," καλυπτειν, which is a "veil" or "covering that hides." Thus, the English translation of "revelation" is literally "to remove the veil" or to "reveal what has been hidden." It is this method of textual unveiling that John chooses in order to express his message.

Generally speaking (and John is no exception here), apocalypses describe the current situation, provide a context, and then place the reader within a specific location of that context in order to clearly show what has previously been unknown/hidden. John begins this process by using a language of vision that directs the readers' gaze down a particular path. Before providing a new revelation, the revelator must necessarily convince the listeners that a new revelation is needed. John (similar to other apocalyptic writers) accomplishes this by describing in some detail the crisis situation of his present. As in the case of John's text, apocalyptic language often includes descriptions of sufferings and violence that elicit a corresponding sense of sadness or anger or empathy in the intended audience. Even when the audience may already be aware of the crisis situation—which almost always prefigures apocalyptic writing—hearing one's experience of oppression provides validation in and of itself. Accordingly, recognition of such a state of sorrow and oppression instills a longing and desire for change within the minds of those who hear. Apocalyptic revelators knew (and know) that change often only comes with disillusionment and, therefore, the disillusionment needs to be rendered before a new revelation will be heard and accepted as motivation for action. As the audience, we follow John's narrative finger to look more clearly on the apocalyptic crisis and to see past the veils of Rome's lure of wealth, arrogance, and oppression (for example, in 18:7, "As she glorified herself and lived luxuriously, so give her a like measure of torment and grief. Since in her heart she says, 'I rule as a queen; I am no widow, and I will never see grief.'").[1]

When Caesar crossed the Rubicon, defying the Senate and the Roman Republic and replacing it with the Empire, he may have begun with the best of intentions, but he also opened the floodgates that would eventually drown the Roman legal, economic, and social systems. Subsequent emperors raised themselves above the law, even to the point of trumping religious law as they claimed divinity and demanded acknowledgement of their divine transformation. As a result, there was no authority to hold them accountable for their actions. As John intimates and as history reveals, an empire is truly dangerous when the violence stems not only from the government breaking laws, but from a government's changing the laws to make the violence legal. Consequently, rather than the "Pax Romana" that the Roman Empire was proclaiming, John reveals the hypocrisy of the Roman Empire; namely, that it has used its wealth to seduce the kings of the earth (see Revelation 17:2; 18:3) and has used its armies to force its inhabitants to participate in their own and others' religious and economic oppression (see Revelation 15:8; 17:18; 19:19).

And, indeed, the economy was governed by religion. No one could trade in the marketplace until they had first paid (literally) honor to the statue of the emperor (or, in John's words, "the beast"). The statues—as the remnants

---

[1] Except as otherwise noted, all scripture references are from the Book of Revelation in the New Revised Standard Version of the Bible.

show in the Middle East today—are hollow, allowing for a representative of the Emperor to step inside and, therefore, "speak" for the Caesar. The representative may have been a priest or government official. The statue would "speak" to either accept or decline the offering. If the offering was accepted, the person could then trade and buy in the marketplace. But if not, the person could be killed or, at the least, refused entry into the market. There are two general interpretations of how people were marked for acceptance with the "mark of the beast" as John calls it. One, is that they were given Roman coins to trade in the market, which would have borne the image of the Caesar as God. The use of these coins may have been seen as blasphemy in the early Christian community. In fact, Jewish zealots who rebelled against Rome in the years before the fall of the Jerusalem temple (66-70 C.E.) did not use, touch, or even look at such coins. Another interpretation reads the text more literally in that the ones whose offerings were accepted were actually marked to show their compliance with the Roman government. Whatever the specific interpretation, the meaning remains the same—those who did not honor/worship the Caesar could not eat or live. Revelation 13 describes this theological-economic crisis as follows:

Then I saw another beast that rose out of the earth... It exercises all the authority of the first beast on its behalf, and it makes the earth and its inhabitants worship the first beast... it deceives the inhabitants of earth, telling them to make an image for the beast... and it was allowed to give breath to the image of the beast so that the image of the

*beast could even speak and cause those who would not
worship the image of the beast to be killed. Also, it causes
all, both small and great, both rich and poor, both free and
slave, to be marked on the right hand or the forehead, so
that no one can buy or sell who does not have the mark,
that is, the name of the beast or the number of its name.
(Revelation 13:11-17)*

This method ensured that the first and best fruits went
to the emperor/beast (or to the emperor's liaison as the
case may be). Thus, not only was the Empire committing
harm, but it was doing so under the guise of peace.

John, however, goes much further than simply
condemning single acts of the Roman Empire, as
idolatrous as they might have been. Drawing on scriptural
texts and images (primarily from Ezekiel, Jeremiah, and
Isaiah, who also condemned exploitative trade and
economic domination), Revelation contains a scathing
visual condemnation of Rome's entire exploitative system,
one that drained the lifeblood from the majority to enable
an affluent, small minority.

Using vivid language and traditional imagery, John
describes Rome as a drunken, bloodthirsty prostitute
adorned with jewels and gold (Revelation 17:1-6). "Roma,"
looking like a goddess but acting the whore, has lured
kings into alliances with her (17:2—no multi-lateral
agreements here) and deceived and seduced her own
people. But now Rome has gone too far, John lifts the veil
on her perfect image and reveals that she is drunk... with
blood. References to drinking blood, thirsting for blood,
and becoming drunk on blood were traditional images for

militancy and violence that are found not only in biblical scriptures (e.g., Isaiah 49:26), but also in extra-biblical sources including Josephus (5.344) and Suetonius (3.59.2).

This critique in Chapter 17 of violence, militarism, and political allegiances is expanded in Chapter 18 to include an additional indictment, that of economic exploitation. And this is where another veil comes tumbling down. As the angel laments, "Fallen, fallen is Babylon (Rome) the great!" (18:2), we hear the laments of those who profited with her and who now mourn their (financial) loss: all the nations, the kings of the earth, and the merchants who grew rich from her luxury (18:3). This entire chapter reveals that Rome's primary crime is its unjust wealth from predatory trade. Rome has used deception (18:23) and corruption (19:2) in order to exploit the masses, who fail to see that they are in fact being exploited.

By verse 22 of Chapter 18, nothing human is left in the city. The repeated phrase "no more" is the hollow echo. No sounds are heard, "and the sound of harpists and minstrels and of flutists and trumpeters will be heard in you no more; and an artisan of any trade will be found in you no more; and the sound of the millstone will be heard in you no more" (18:22). No light remains, "and the light of a lamp will shine in you no more" (18:23); no sign of rites of passage, "and the voice of bridegroom and bride will be heard in you no more" (18:23). Ironically, the only life Rome has left is the lifeblood of the prophets and saints and others who were killed. ("And in you was found the blood of prophets and of saints, and of all who have been slaughtered on earth." 18:24) This satirical lament (most evident for its lack of a conclusion calling for restoration) has a dual purpose: to show the coming destruction of the destroyer Babylon/Rome and to issue a call to the audience.

Last Call

Surprisingly, John does not go ahead in Chapter 18 with the traditionally expected details of war and judgment for a condemned city. In fact, such a battle never happens in this text. Rather, John immediately describes the details of the city's devastation. Literally, the city falls for its sins, for the oppression and exploitation of the weak and impoverished. This type of devastation is also a sign of empire. Where a city is protected and even known by its city wall, the Roman Empire, by contrast, has, according to the Roman historian, Aelius Aristides, no need for walls since the "whole inhabited world" is under its control. Rome was protected not by "bitumen and baked brick," but by its people. Consequently, when it falls in the text, it is not from an external battle that breaks through a breach in the city wall, rather true destruction can only be from an internal collapse. This also means that the empire is maintained by the people, for the people. And this is why John issues his call before the empire collapses in on itself.

It is significant at this point to mention what may be a primary difference between a prophetic and apocalyptic call for change. Prophecy, certainly, calls for reform of the current social order. Apocalypses, however, challenge their readers to re-examine and question the core values on which the society runs... and dare their readers to create a new world. Just when John has his readers in the palm of his hand, with his diatribe against the evil Roman Empire and its oppression of his audience culminating in the political critique of Chapter 17 (and just when the audience is feeling piously self-righteous), John issues his specific challenge. And the last veil drops. "Come out of her my people, so that you do not take part in her sins, and so that you do not share in her plagues; for her sins are heaped high as heaven, and God has remembered her iniquities" (18:5). Shockingly, we the readers are among those deceived by Rome. We ourselves partake in the Empire's economic system. And, any participation in the Roman economic system, even by those who are oppressed, is supporting the system, and thereby supporting the Empire.

Apocalyptic language is often concerned with identity, generally within the context of identifying who is experiencing the crisis situation (I, we), and who is imposing the crisis (they, the enemy, the other). John turns this identification inside out as he reveals that "we" are indeed part of "them," since we are participating in their economy. In addition, John suggests that not only will the government be held accountable, but all who reside within the borders of the Empire will be held accountable as well, since anyone who "resides in her" will "take part." John's strident challenge to refuse to participate in oppressive social, economic, and political ventures comes at the cost of losing not only property, but privilege and credibility.

It may be worthwhile to note here that the interpretations of the Book of Revelation are often understood as falling into two broad camps. First, are those interpretations that understand John's message as pertaining to the future... and that future is now. They interpret the beast and Babylon according to whomever their political rival is at the time (current favorites include Saddam Hussein, Osama bin Laden, and George W. Bush to name a few), and the various references to violence in the Book are played out accordingly. Second, are those who believe that John was writing about the Roman Empire only and, therefore, the audience and interpretation of the text is limited to the first and second century listeners.

There is, however, a third camp that incorporates the Quaker emphasis on spiritual context. This interpretation views the themes of exile and community (including the realities of empire and economic oppression) as ongoing human experiences, and seeks to understand how we may incorporate the knowledge into our own lives. Rather than attempting to identify, for example, a modern day person as "the beast," this interpretation recognizes that there are empires that rise and fall, and that many governments exploit and oppress. This latter interpretation calls for the readers of Revelation to see how they may be participating in the oppression of the current embodiment of Empire, and to remove themselves from that participation.

Stripping away this final veil reveals the hard truth of the sacrifice required to end hierarchy and oppression and to bring about justice and mercy, the truth of exile and community, of hate and love, of violence and peace, of hell and heaven—the truth of being estranged from the sacred, divine "Being," from our experience of "Being," from our own being, from being human/humane. John's vision is an eschatological end to the present oppressive order, a vision of hope, a vision of the end and beginning, of death and life.

To carry John's argument to its logical conclusion, all who continue to participate in the beast's inhumane affairs are in danger of becoming inhuman/beastly themselves as injustice and oppression continue to rule. This is particularly poignant if we bring ourselves to substitute Rome with something closer to home. The American Empire has grown in wealth and military force in recent years. As an American citizen, it is difficult for me to read this apocalyptic text without hearing its enduring truth about "empires," military force, economic oppression and political posturing.

John is pointing us toward our responsibility, toward those necessary though difficult questions of how we participate in the world, our communities, and our families. He provides a chance to consider which of our choices are encouraging community and which ones, exile. Perhaps his revelation of choice is "some of the hidden manna" promised to those who "hear what the Spirit says" and "overcome" (2:17). I need John's glimpse behind the veil to remind me that I have the ability to choose differently, to choose to live from and with truth and integrity, turning away from the hollow beast.

Additional Reading

Collins, Adela Yarbro. *The Apocalypse*. Collegeville, Minnesota: The Liturgical Press, 1990.

Collins, John J. *Apocalypticism in the Dead Sea Scrolls*. New York: Routledge, 1977.

- Collins has a good, general description of "apocalypticism" in Chapter 1.

O'Leary, Stephen. *Arguing the Apocalypse*. New York: Oxford University Press, 1994.

- O'Leary presents an interesting analysis of apocalypse as rhetorical argument in his book by looking at studies of apocalyptic movements.

Ochs, Carol. *Our Lives as Torah: Finding God in our own Stories*. San Francisio: Jossey-Bass, 2001.

Remen, Rachel Naomi. *Kitchen Table Wisdom: Stories that Heal*. New York: Riverhead Books, 1996.

Meeks, Wayne A. (ed). *The HarperCollins Study Bible, with the Apocryphal/Deuterocanonical Books*. New York: Harper Collins Publisher, 1993.

- This study Bible is quite good at providing the English translations for personal names, place names, and general literary background information.

CPSIA information can be obtained at www.ICGtesting.com
Printed in the USA
LVOW101744160712

290293LV00007B/74/A